Overcoming Chronic Fatigue in Young People

Overcoming Chronic Fatigue in Young People provides an effective evidence-based, step-by-step guide to managing and overcoming chronic fatigue. The highly-experienced experts in the field, Katharine Rimes and Trudie Chalder, present an accessible and practical manual aimed at young people, with downloadable material (available online) to support recovery. The book also includes a guide for parents and a helpful resources section. It is recommended for any young person struggling with chronic fatigue, as well as parents and professionals.

Currently, there is no other evidence-based self-help guide available on chronic fatigue aimed at young people. This innovative book contains detailed advice for tailoring a fatigue recovery programme to the individual and shows the health professional how to do this. Topics covered include: sleep, exercise, coping with stress and school. Based on cognitive behaviour therapy, a treatment approach supported by research evidence, Katharine Rimes and Trudie Chalder have used this guide in specialist CFS/ME service for many years with positive results as reported by both patients and parents.

Overcoming Chronic Fatigue in Young People is aimed at young people with CFS/ME but people with chronic fatigue caused by other conditions will also find it invaluable. It is an essential resource for parents, families and health care professionals in the treatment of their clients.

Dr Katharine Rimes is a chartered clinical and health psychologist who has worked with people with chronic fatigue and CFS/ME in the National Health Service for over fifteen years. She is an accredited cognitive behaviour therapist. She also works as a senior university lecturer and has published many research titles about CFS/ME.

Professor Trudie Chalder is a world expert in chronic fatigue and CFS/ME. She and colleagues developed the cognitive behavioural treatment of CFS/ME and fatigue in the context of other medical conditions. She is Professor of Cognitive Behavioural Psychotherapy at King's College London, and a health psychologist and cognitive behaviour therapist who has worked with fatigued individuals for 27 years. She has been widely published.

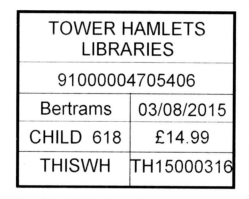

Overcoming Chronic Fatigue in Young People

A cognitive-behavioural self-help guide

Katharine Rimes
and Trudie Chalder

Routledge
Taylor & Francis Group

LONDON AND NEW YORK

First published 2016
by Routledge
27 Church Road, Hove, East Sussex, BN3 2FA

And by Routledge
711 Third Avenue, New York, NY 10017

Routledge is an imprint of the Taylor & Francis Group, an informa business

The self-help instructions in this book are for use under the guidance of a health professional. You should see your general practitioner if you have been experiencing fatigue for at least three months that is causing problems for your everyday activities. No responsibility can be accepted for the consequences of the unsupervised application of the suggestions in this book.

British Library Cataloguing in Publication Data
A catalogue record for this book is available from the British Library

Library of Congress Cataloging-in-Publication Data
Rimes, Katharine.
Overcoming chronic fatigue in young people : a cognitive-behavioural self-help guide / Katharine Rimes and Trudie Chalder.
pages cm
1. Fatigue—Treatment—Popular works. 2. Chronic fatigue syndrome—Treatment—Popular works. 3. Myalgic encephalomyelitis—Treatment—Popular works. 4. Youth—Health and hygiene—Popular works. 5. Cognitive therapy—Popular works. I. Chalder, Trudie. II. Title.
RB150.F37.R56 2015
616'.0478—dc23
2015002425

ISBN: 978-1-138-80288-9 (hbk)
ISBN: 978-1-138-80289-6 (pbk)
ISBN: 978-1-315-74830-6 (ebk)

Typeset in New Century Schoolbook
by Apex CoVantage, LLC
Printed and bound by Ashford Colour Press Ltd., Gosport, Hampshire

MIX
Paper from
responsible sources
FSC
www.fsc.org   FSC® C011748

Contents

Acknowledgements

We would like to thank the children and parents who have given us feedback on this guide, as well as South London and Maudsley Trust (Research and Development) for funding research about an intervention using this guide.

We would like to acknowledge:

Vincent Deary for his contribution to a previous draft of the self-help guide;

Trudie Chalder and Kaneez Hussain, *Self-help for Chronic Fatigue Syndrome – a guide for young people* (Witney, UK: Blue Stallion Publications, 2002);

Mary Burgess and Trudie Chalder, *Overcoming chronic fatigue* (London: Robinson, 2005);

Pauline Powell, *Chronic Fatigue Syndrome: What you need to get better* (unpublished manuscript).

Acknowledgments

What is chronic fatigue and chronic fatigue syndrome/ME?

All of us feel tired at times, but if you feel tired a lot of the time, you might have a condition called chronic fatigue syndrome (CFS). Some people call it ME (myalgic encephalomyelitis) or post-viral fatigue syndrome. Different people prefer different names, and for simplicity we will for the rest of this book use the term CFS/ME. CFS/ME refers to a condition where you feel very tired most of the time and have felt this way for at least three months (or six months if you are an adult). In addition to physical and mental fatigue, you may have problems concentrating, problems with your memory, or problems finding the right word. You may have other symptoms, such as muscle pain, headaches and sleep problems. Resting may not relieve the tiredness.

For a doctor to decide that you have CFS/ME, he or she will first carry out routine investigations to find the cause of your fatigue. If no medical problem is found which may be making you feel like this, and you have been checked by a paediatrician, your doctor may diagnose you with CFS/ME.

As you can see, the name *describes* your condition. *Chronic* means long term, *fatigue* is another word for tiredness and a *syndrome* is a particular group of symptoms that together form an illness. The name is neutral in that it doesn't imply that there is a cause for the illness. This is deliberate, as a specific cause for CFS/ME has not been found. CFS/ME is a controversial condition, and some people do not believe that it is a real illness. We know that people with CFS/ME really are ill, but we believe that they can be helped.

If your symptoms are not severe enough to be classified as CFS/ME, you may still be experiencing 'chronic fatigue' if your fatigue has been around for several months. The ideas in this book may be useful for you even if you have not been diagnosed with CFS/ME.

This guide

You may have already received different types of advice about how to get better. This can be upsetting and confusing, on top of you already feeling unwell.

This guide is based on a self-help programme that our research has found to be helpful for young people with CFS/ME. It is based on ideas from cognitive behaviour therapy (CBT), which research has demonstrated to be an effective treatment for CFS/ME in young people. This type of intervention can help reduce fatigue, reduce the problems it can cause in different areas of life, and increase school attendance. This guide is intended mainly for young people between the ages of 10 and 18 years, but it could be useful for people older or younger than this.

Why did you get it?

Nobody really knows why people get CFS/ME. It can start after an illness, such as flu or glandular fever; after a stressful experience, such as working very hard for exams; or after a big life change, such as going to a new school.

Following are some examples of things that can contribute to the development of CFS/ME.

- **Physical factors** such as infections or anaemia. An initial illness is often reported as a trigger for the fatigue. However, there is no clear evidence of a virus or bacteria remaining in the body and causing the ongoing symptoms once the chronic fatigue or CFS/ME has become established.
- **Stress.** Stress can be caused by anything, such as worries about school or friends, a bereavement, family problems and so on. There is increasing evidence of a link between stress and the immune system not working as well as it should. (The 'immune system' refers to the parts of the body that work to fight off infection.)
- **Having very high expectations of oneself.** If you are always pushing yourself hard to achieve well or to do things 'perfectly', this can cause stress, frustration and fatigue.

- **Very high levels of exercise.** Training excessively hard can actually make the immune system work less well, making you vulnerable to infection and fatigue. Also, if you are very physically fit your body will lose its strength much more quickly when you are forced to rest (e.g. through illness) compared to someone who isn't very fit to begin with. This means that you are more likely to notice feeling weaker or tiring more easily compared to a previous time when you had to rest.
- **Busy lifestyle.** Fatigue can develop in people who have a very busy lifestyle because they do not leave enough time for rest and relaxation.

Just because factors such as stress can trigger CFS/ME does not mean that the symptoms are 'all in your mind'. Your mind and body are constantly influencing each other. The chances of developing any illness, from a common cold to a heart attack, can be influenced by stress levels, moods, attitudes and so on.

Examples of how fatigue problems can develop

Sunita

Sunita developed CFS/ME in the months before her mock GCSEs. She felt that everyone was expecting her to do really well, and she was determined not to let herself or other people down. She was under a lot of pressure and worked as hard as she could, cutting down on her usual hobbies and relaxation activities. She was pushing herself as hard as she could, but she was barely coping. The thing that pushed her over the edge was the death of her grandfather. After his death Sunita felt that she no longer had any motivation or energy left, and she became more and more fatigued. In this example there was a combination of both chronic stress and bereavement that led to CFS/ME.

Harry

Harry was always good at sports and was on his school's teams for rugby and swimming. He loved training and did some form of sports or exercise every day. When he got a virus he rested in bed for days, which he hated, so he returned to his sports as soon as he could. But he found that he couldn't perform as well as before. He experienced muscle and joint pain and didn't have as much energy or strength as before. So he tried resting some more to get his strength back. But when he again returned to his sports activities the same thing happened – more muscle and joint pain and less strength. He tried pushing himself really hard to train his body to its earlier levels, but this just made him so exhausted that he had to spend several days in bed. Eventually he stopped playing any sports, but the muscle and joint pains continued and the fatigue got worse. In Harry's case we see someone who was extremely fit and whose CFS/ME was triggered by a virus.

Your own case may be quite different from these two. Do you think that any of the factors discussed in these cases may be relevant in your situation?

The good news is that we don't have to have a complete understanding of *why* your fatigue was triggered in order to help you get over it. This is partly because the factors that triggered your fatigue are not necessarily the same as those that keep it going. Those factors will be discussed in the next section.

What keeps CFS/ME going?

A number of things are likely to have been involved in the development of CFS/ME, but it's likely that once it has been triggered different factors keep the fatigue and disability going. The following sections list some of the reasons. See if any seem true in your case.

Returning to normal activities too soon after initial infection

Sometimes people have tried to keep up with their usual levels of exercise or other activities despite being in the early stages of a serious virus that may include having a fever. Or they have returned to their previous activity levels too quickly without taking into account that they have been ill. This can make them feel worse. It is important to rest or 'take it easy' during an *acute* illness. However, resting too much may also slow down or get in the way of recovery, as will be discussed in the following section.

Resting too much

If you've been ill for a while, and have cut down on your activities, your body will not be used to doing much and it will be less fit in a number of ways. Your muscles will be weaker and will produce less energy because they haven't been used as much, leaving you with less stamina. If you suddenly try to do more, your muscles will hurt. This is not because of muscle disease but because they are out of condition.

The physical effects of rest and inactivity are discussed further in the section 'Why focus on activities?' in chapter 3 of this book.

See-sawing or 'boom and bust'

You may be see-sawing between doing a lot on a 'good' day and then feeling worse afterwards and having to rest a lot. Then you might start to feel better and push yourself too far again. This overactivity/underactivity pattern (sometimes called 'boom and bust') can become a cycle that's hard to get out of. Through this process your body can end up getting weaker rather than stronger. It's important to keep a balance between rest and activity every day.

Disrupted routines

It's also important to stick to a similar routine every day. Not sticking to a regular routine can upset the timing of your so-called body clock, which controls rhythms in your body. This can make you feel generally unwell, with symptoms such as headaches, poor concentration and alertness, low energy and poor-quality sleep.

Being afraid of making things worse

You and your parents may understandably be afraid of making the fatigue worse. You may have been given different advice from different doctors about how to cope with fatigue. It wouldn't be surprising if you feel confused about whether an activity may harm your body or make you worse. Perhaps when you have tried to go back to your normal activities the fatigue has gotten worse. It seems sensible to rest when you're tired, but this only helps for a little while. Rest does not help illnesses that have lasted a long time. In fact, the more you rest the more fatigued you will feel.

Being too tough on yourself

You may have previously played a lot of sports or you were used to doing lots of activities. You might be expecting yourself to get better and return to that level of activity very quickly. During a period of rest, fit and active people lose more fitness than unfit people simply because they have more to lose. They therefore need longer than unfit people do to return to their previous fitness level. Maybe you are pushing yourself too hard and are expecting changes too quickly. During your recovery period, don't expect to perform at your previous level. It will take time and practice to return to normal.

Research has shown that young people with CFS/ME and their parents underestimate how active they have actually been! They also underestimate how tired healthy adolescents actually get. Do what you can manage and don't give yourself a hard time.

Sleep disturbance

Sleeping problems can also help keep the fatigue going. For example, when you are fatigued it is tempting to sleep or rest in the daytime to try to make yourself feel better. Alternatively, you may adjust your bedtime according to how fatigued you feel. Unfortunately this has the effect of disrupting your nighttime sleep and your normal body rhythms. Too much sleep can actually make you feel worse rather than better, because the sleep is often 'light' and not refreshing.

Conflicting advice

Many families tell us that they have been given little helpful advice, advice that is too vague and non-specific or conflicting advice from different health professionals. Unfortunately, because the CBT treatment for CFS/ME in children is new, many doctors have not heard that it can be effective and they will not always know what to advise. Some families feel that they have received little support, which has added to their stress levels.

Focusing on symptoms

When you've had a symptom for a long time it's understandable that you will be worried about it. The more something worries us, the more we notice it and pay attention to it. Focusing on the symptoms can make them seem worse, can make you feel more stressed and can result in you not having enough 'spare' attention for other things that are going on.

Feeling frustrated or low

You may feel low at times, and this is to be expected because CFS/ME is a distressing condition. You may feel that you can't do anything about your fatigue and that you don't know why it's happening or how long it will last. Feeling frustrated or low can drain your energy further.

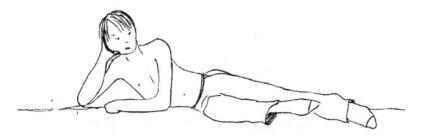

Worries

Not doing things regularly makes you lose confidence in yourself. You may be worried, for example, about going back to school, about what you've missed or that your friends are moving on without you. This can mean double trouble – you have to cope with these worries *and* the CFS/ME. Again these worries will make you feel worse.

Summary of how CFS/ME can develop

Stress or an infection can leave you feeling tired. It is normal to rest or to cut down on activities in response to tiredness. However, if you rest too much or if your body loses its fitness you will feel more tired than usual when you return to your usual activities, and you may have symptoms such as dizziness and muscle pain.

If resting has meant that your sleep pattern has changed, your body clock may have been disrupted. Because of the effects on your body you will find it harder to perform normal activities.

If you experience unpleasant symptoms upon returning to normal activities, you may lose confidence. You may worry that you will never be able to do the things you used to. The frustration and worry also contribute to feeling tired and lacking energy.

Alternatively, you may have had a very busy lifestyle or were doing a great deal of sport or exercise, which you have been trying to keep up with despite being unwell. Doing too much may have put you at greater risk of becoming unwell with severe fatigue. If this is the case then it will be important to have a more balanced lifestyle with time for rest and relaxation.

The following sections provide more information about how we think your CFS/ME may have started and then carried on. We will also show you how to tackle the factors that may be keeping it going.

Help is on the way!

What is cognitive behaviour therapy?

This guide is based on a treatment called cognitive behaviour therapy (CBT). The word *cognitive* means 'how you think' and *behaviour* means 'what you do'. Following this guide may help you do things differently and perhaps think a little differently – this will make you feel differently as well. We've found that CBT helps people with CFS/ME and is completely safe. It is used successfully for managing other illnesses as well, such as diabetes. This guide may help you work out the problems of CFS/ME and help you regain the confidence which is often lost when people have this type of illness. You will have to do some homework on your own, such as keeping a diary. Sorry if it sounds as though you're at school!

Be patient – CBT is not an overnight remedy. It takes time and you will have to work at it with the help of your family or friends. Your mum, dad, brothers and sisters can benefit by learning and practising a little CBT themselves while helping you along the way!

Research into CBT with adults with CFS/ME

Research involving adults with CFS/ME has shown that CBT helps with fatigue, other symptoms of CFS/ME and functioning. In a research study, 70 per cent of the adults who completed their CBT programme were better able to do physical tasks and activities, and they remained improved six months after they finished treatment.

These patients were contacted five years after their treatment to see how they were doing. Again, almost 70 per cent of the adults who received CBT said they were better. Most of the patients felt good about the CBT and still used some of the techniques they had learned.

Results of our pilot study of CBT and young people with CFS/ME

A smaller study of young people with CFS/ME who used CBT found that after treatment, the majority of participants were less tired and were attending school at least 75 per cent of the time. After six months, all of the young people who completed their CBT programme were back at school and 95 per cent were attending full time. As well as feeling less tired, most of the young people reported improvements in their social lives, fears and depression.

Although CBT is not a cure for CFS/ME, the research described here shows that it can reduce the symptoms of CFS/ME and can help people return to their normal activities, thus improving their well-being and quality of life. These improvements seem to be long term.

If you persevere and be positive you will get better!

What will it involve?

1 **Charting your activity levels**
   Completing your daily activity diaries will help you build a
   picture of what you are doing each day. You will be able
   to see more easily whether there are times when you are
   doing too much or too little.

2 **Setting targets**
   Targets will be varied (e.g. not just about school) in order to
   make your life as balanced as possible. The targets will
   help you focus on what *you* would like to work towards
   during the next few months.

3 **Getting into a routine of activity and rest**
   This will involve planning a programme of activity and rest.
   The aim is to carry out the same amount of activity and
   rest each day to avoid bursts of activity when feeling well
   and long periods of rest when fatigued.

4 **Increasing or changing your activities**
   When you have established a routine, including planned activity and rest, you will take steps to gradually increase some

activities (e.g. exercise or sport) and reintroduce activities that you had to stop because of your fatigue.

5 **Getting into a regular sleep routine**

How you do this will depend on the sleep problems you may have. It may include cutting out sleep during the day, reducing sleep at night and/or having a regular bedtime and wake-up time.

6 **Learning to overcome unhelpful thoughts and beliefs**

This will involve identifying thoughts such as 'I'll never get better' or 'I haven't achieved anything today'. These may be slowing down your progress and may result in feelings of frustration. You will then learn to challenge these thoughts by coming up with more helpful alternatives.

7 **Learning how to keep up your gains and make further progress**

This will involve getting a better understanding of your illness (especially the factors that keep it going), learning how to address these problem areas and learning how to continue to work towards your long-term goals (e.g. starting college). In addition, you will learn how to deal with potential problems.

2

Sleep management

People with CFS/ME often have problems sleeping. You may find it hard to go to sleep, you may wake up during the night or you may need a lot of sleep. When you wake up you may feel exhausted and still feel sleepy during the day. Your sleep patterns may vary a lot from day to day.

Sleep diaries

Completing a sleep diary for a few weeks will help you build a picture of your sleep pattern. This information will help you come up with a sleep programme.

The following is an example of a blank diary, which you can photocopy or use as necessary.

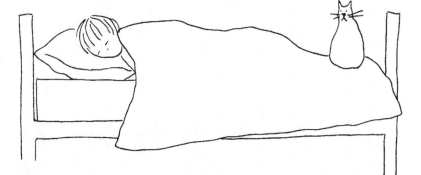

Sleep diary

Photocopy this page and fill it in every morning.

Guess the time it takes you to fall asleep and how long you are awake during the night.

	Example	Monday	Tuesday	Wednesday	Thursday	Friday	Saturday	Sunday
1 I went to bed at ___ o'clock and turned the lights out at ___ o'clock.	10:30pm 11:15pm							
2 After turning the lights out I fell asleep in ___ minutes.	60							
3 My sleep was interrupted ___ times. (Write the number of times you remember waking during the night.)	2							
4 My sleep was interrupted for ___ minutes. (Write how long you were awake each time you woke up.)	20 40							
5 I woke up at ___ o'clock (the last time you woke up).	7:15am							
6 I got out of bed for the day at ___ o'clock.	8:10am							
7 Overall, my sleep was ___ (0 = very sound, 8 = very restless).	6							
8 When I got up this morning I felt ___ (0 = refreshed, 8 = exhausted).	7							
9 In total I slept ___ hours.	6							

The body clock

Our sleep is controlled by a body clock that also controls other rhythms in your body, such as appetite, body temperature and alertness. The clock needs to be reset each day by signals your body produces such as wake-up times and bedtimes, meal times, activities and exercise.

What happens if it slips?

If your body does not receive these cues, such as regular bedtimes, the timing of its rhythms starts to slip. This can cause a number of unpleasant symptoms.

In a study where the sleep patterns of healthy volunteers were disrupted on purpose to mimic the patterns of those with CFS/ME, the volunteers developed symptoms similar to those of CFS/ME, including feeling unrefreshed and physically weak and experiencing sleepiness, poor concentration and muscle aches. However, when they were allowed to sleep undisturbed, their symptoms went away. This study shows that a disturbed sleep pattern can cause some of the symptoms seen in CFS/ME and that these symptoms can be reversed.

Sleep problems can affect the activity of the immune system, possibly increasing the risk of illness and infection.

Why does it slip?

Your body clock can easily be disrupted by staying up too late and sleeping in, sleeping during the day or not being active enough during the day. Perhaps your body clock has been disrupted by you taking more rest in response to an infection or illness or being kept awake at night by stress.

Not having a regular routine, such as going to bed and getting up at different times each day, taking catnaps during the day or even sleeping too much, can disturb your body clock.

Sleeping during the day

Although it may seem like the sensible thing to do because it makes you feel better in the short term, coping with disrupted sleep or tiredness by sleeping during the day does not help. It reduces the quality of your nighttime sleep and further confuses your body clock.

How to reset your body clock and make your sleep better

• Make a 'bedtime-uptime' routine

Get up at the same time every day. Use an alarm clock – put it on the other side of the room so that you have to get up to switch it off. This will help you avoid constantly pressing the snooze button. Or you may want to ask one of your parents to wake you up. Draw back your curtains to let in the light. *Get up at the same time no matter what time you went to bed or how much sleep you had the previous night.* If your sleep is very disrupted you may have to do this gradually by setting for yourself a slightly earlier time to get up each week. The next section explains how to do this.

You should aim to sleep for only about eight hours a night. Sleeping more than this makes you feel sluggish and makes you feel like you need even more sleep. Don't go to bed if you're not feeling tired. There is no need to have a set bedtime, although once you have established a set getting-up time, you may find that you start to get tired at about the same time each evening.

• Don't sleep during the day

If this is a habit of yours you might want to cut down your daytime sleep gradually by reducing it every week. The next section explains how to do this.

• Use your bed only for sleeping

Don't watch TV or read in bed. Try not to use it during the day. Your bed will then become a cue only for sleep. If you've been in bed for more than 20 minutes and haven't fallen asleep, go to another room and do something relaxing until you feel sleepy again. Do this as many times as you have to. It will help you associate your bed only with sleeping. Do the same thing if you wake up in the night and can't get back to sleep right away.

Improving the quality of your sleep

Using your sleep diary, work out how long on average you spend actually asleep at night. For example, you may spend 10 hours in bed each night but only sleep for six hours. To make your sleep efficient, so you don't spend time lying awake in bed, only

spend the average number of hours in bed that you are actually asleep. So if you sleep on average for six hours a night, only spend six hours in bed whether you have slept for six hours or not. You may feel as if you haven't slept enough or you may feel tired the next morning. But if you stick to it, this method will make your sleep deeper and less broken and you will fall asleep faster. Once you have achieved this better-quality sleep you can increase the time you spend asleep up to eight hours.

Sleeping too much

With CFS/ME the more you sleep, the more tired you may feel. It is not unusual for people with CFS/ME to report sleeping up to 12 hours or more. The fact that they are able to sleep so long but still feel tired simply makes them believe even more strongly that this amount of sleep must be needed. However, just because they can sleep for 12 hours does not mean they actually need that much sleep. On the odd occasion that you have missed a lot of sleep it can be okay to sleep more than usual. But if you are sleeping for a very long time every night, this may actually be worsening the fatigue.

The effects of sleeping too much include loss of energy and drive when awake, increased need for sleep, problems with concentration and a reduction in enjoyment and satisfaction with life.

If you are sleeping too much you should try to gradually cut down on your sleep, either by getting up earlier or by going to bed later. It is best to either get up at the same time each morning or go to bed at the same time every night.

For example, if you have been getting up at mid-day, you may want to move this to 11:00am for one or two weeks. When you feel comfortable with this, try getting up at 10:00am, then 9:00am and so on until you are sleeping the amount of time you are happy with. Don't go to bed earlier to make up for the fact that you are getting up earlier!

Getting ready for bed

An hour before bed try to wind down and relax – don't study or exercise, but watch TV or have a warm bath or read. Do things in the same order before going to bed. These will become signals to your body that you're getting ready for sleep.

Improving your chances of a good night's sleep

• Avoid exercise within three hours of bedtime because the activity may wake you up.
• Only have light snacks before bedtime.
• Avoid snacking in the middle of the night.
• Limit drinks before bedtime – too much fluid may mean that you wake up to go to the toilet and then have problems returning to sleep.
• Avoid drinks with caffeine (e.g. Coca-Cola, coffee, tea) within four to six hours of bedtime.
• Make sure your bedroom is a comfortable temperature.
• Wear earplugs if noise is a problem.
• Make sure your bed and mattress are comfortable.

Can't sleep?

If you go to bed and find that you can't fall asleep, try these tricks.

• Don't start worrying about not being able to fall asleep. Reassure yourself that 'sleep will come when it's ready' and 'relaxing in bed is almost as good'.

- Keep your eyes open in the dark and try to keep them open even as you begin to feel sleepy.
- Imagine a pleasant scene where you are feeling relaxed and peaceful.
- Relax the different areas of your body one by one, and breathe slowly and deeply.
- If you haven't fallen asleep in 20 minutes or find that you're not sleepy anymore, get up and go to another room until you feel sleepy again.

How to reduce worrying at night

If you can't sleep because you keep worrying, make yourself a Worry Time. This can be a slot during the day when you can think and talk about any worries you have and what you can do to alleviate them. Sometimes it helps to write them down. You may want to use the problem-solving method described in chapter 5. If you find yourself worrying in bed, tell yourself you'll deal with the problem during Worry Time.

Sleep management – final comments

You may wonder why you have to stick to these rules about going to sleep while other people do not. But if you are suffering

from unpleasant symptoms because of a disturbed sleep routine, this is the only way to relieve them.

Changing your habits will be difficult but sticking with these rules will mean that in a few weeks you will not have to suffer from the symptoms caused by a disrupted body clock. You may feel worse to begin with and you may find that you are not sleeping very much. Don't sleep during the day to make up for it. After a few weeks of sticking to these rules you will begin to feel better and your sleep will improve. As you incorporate more activity and exercise into your routine, you will find that the quality of your sleep improves further.

3

Activity scheduling

How to complete activity diaries

Activity diaries are very important because they help you get an accurate picture of how you are spending your time. They will also make it easier to see what changes you would like to make. Once you have started treatment, the diaries will help demonstrate your progress and will highlight any areas of difficulty.

For each hour jot down what you are doing, even if it is 'doing nothing'.

Record your activities at regular intervals throughout the day. If you leave it to the end of the day, the task may seem too big to complete and you may forget some of the details.

This chapter includes an example of a completed activity diary and a blank activity diary that you can photocopy.

You may wish to make up your own form on a computer if it would be easier to complete that way.

Why focus on activities?

One thing that those diagnosed with CFS/ME have in common is a difficulty keeping up with their previous activities. They may have to rest during or between activities or even give up some of their previous activities.

Although people often rest and reduce their activities in order to try to feel better, this may actually be counterproductive. In other words, resting and reducing activities can keep the fatigue going rather than relieve it. The following section describes why this is the case.

Physical effects of rest and reduced activity

Over time, reduced activity and increased periods of rest cause physical changes in muscles and in the body's systems. These

Weekly activity schedule

Example of a completed form

	Monday	Tuesday	Wednesday	Thursday	Friday	Saturday	Sunday
7–8	Asleep	Asleep	Asleep	Asleep	Woke 7:30	Asleep	Asleep
8–9	Asleep	Asleep	Asleep	Woke 8:30 Listened to radio	Got up 8:30 Breakfast	Asleep	Asleep
9–10	Asleep	Woke 9:00 Lay in bed	Asleep	Got up Breakfast	Shower, dressed Watched TV	Woke 9:30 Breakfast	Asleep
10–11	Woke 10:00 Breakfast	Breakfast Radio	Asleep	Shower, dressed Internet	Did maths exercises	Shower, dressed	Woke 10:30
11–12	Watched TV	Walked to corner shop	Woke 11:00 Breakfast	Tried reading book for English	Rested Listened to radio	Watched Sarah swimming in race	Breakfast Shower, dressed
12–1	Read book for English	Rested Read magazine	Shower, dressed	Tidied bedroom	Walked to corner shop	Watched swimming race	Went to Gran's house
1–2	Lunch	Lunch Internet	Supermarket with mum	Lunch Watched TV	Lunch Watched TV	Went home	Lunch with Gran

2–3	Slept	Tried to read English book	Supermarket Lunch	Played piano half hour Rested	Helped mum on computer	Lunch	Watched TV at Gran's
3–4	Slept	Slept	Tried maths exercises	Watched TV	Slept	Slept	Slept on Gran's bed
4–5	Talked to Sarah	Tried book again	Slept	Slept	Nicki phoned	Slept	Went home
5–6	Phoned Nicki	Helped Simon with homework	Watched TV	Slept	Did some drawing	Texted friends Watched TV	Computer games
6–7	Internet	Watched TV	Dinner	Helped mum with dinner Rested, dinner	Internet 15 mins Rested	Watched TV	Did some drawing
7–8	Dinner Watched TV	Internet 15 mins Dinner	Asked dad about maths	Dinner Talked to Sarah	Dinner Talked to dad and mum	Dinner	Dinner Watched TV
8–9	Watched TV	Watched videos on Internet	Internet	Computer games	Watched TV	Watched film	Watched TV
9–10	Listened to music Read magazine	Computer games	Watched TV Talked to Sarah	Listened to music	Watched TV	Watched film	Bath Bed 9:30
10–11	Bed 10:30	Bed 10:00	Bed 10:00	Bed 10:00	Bed 11:00	Bed 11:00	Asleep

Weekly activity schedule

Week beginning _____

	Monday	Tuesday	Wednesday	Thursday	Friday	Saturday	Sunday
7–8							
8–9							
9–10							
10–11							
11–12							
12–1							
1–2							
2–3							
3–4							
4–5							
5–6							
6–7							
7–8							
8–9							
9–10							
10–11							

changes cause unpleasant sensations and symptoms, but they are not abnormal or unnatural. They are the ways in which the body tries to adjust to unfavourable conditions.

Research has found that there are many similarities between those with CFS/ME and healthy individuals who have reduced their activities and increased their rest. The following are some of the effects of long periods of inactivity on the body. It is important to point out that these changes are reversible.

1 **Changes in muscle function**
   • People with CFS/ME have been shown to have changes within the cells in their muscles that healthy, active people do not have. These changes may account for feeling a lack of power or energy in the muscles. The same changes have also been found in people without CFS/ME who are inactive. This evidence indicates that the muscle changes in those with CFS/ME are not the cause of the condition but are the consequence of increased rest and reduced activity levels.

2 **Reduced ability to exercise**
   • When muscles are not used regularly they become unfit or deconditioned. When these muscles are then used again during activity there may be feelings of fatigue, weakness, heaviness and instability followed by delayed pain and discomfort. There may also be an increase in overall fatigue after exercise.
   • In everyone, muscle pain and stiffness is a natural consequence of doing exercise that the body isn't used to.

3 **Changes in the cardiovascular system**
   • The cardiovascular system (which includes the heart and blood vessels) becomes out of condition very quickly with increased rest. The longer you rest, the more changes occur.
   • Physical changes that occur include
      • reduced blood volume after one or two days of bed rest,
      • reduced volume of red blood cells after eight days of bed rest,
      • heart muscle deconditions and there is reduced capacity of the heart by about 15 per cent after 20 days of bed rest.

   These physical changes may result in you feeling breathless or dizzy when exercising and they may contribute to your fatigue.
   • Following a 'lying down' rest there is a drop in blood pressure upon standing up. This can cause dizziness and sometimes fainting when you stand up.

4 **Body temperature problems**
   • Long periods of rest lead to changes in the way that blood flows to the major organs of the body. This can result in changes in body temperature so that you tend to feel hot or cold, sometimes with increased sweating.
5 **Clumsiness and coordination problems**
   • Regular performance of an activity is required to maintain good coordination.
   • Prolonged periods of inactivity therefore reduce coordination, which may result in unsteadiness and clumsiness.
6 **Alteration of the biological clock**
   • Part of the brain (the hypothalamus) regulates body rhythms that run on an approximately 24-hour cycle. These rhythms are called 'circadian rhythms' and are responsible for your body 'feeling' things at certain times of the day – for example, hunger, alertness, tiredness, needing to go to the toilet and so on.
   • The biological clock is affected by the events of the day and is reset each day by cues such as waking up or falling asleep, eating meals and performing other daily routines.
   • The biological clock's time-keeping can be disturbed if not reset by these cues in situations such as flying across different time zones (jet lag), working night shifts or experiencing illness.
   • Disruption of the clock results in a slipping of body rhythms that can lead to
      • the 'normal' intense feelings of tiredness at night shifting into the day, making it difficult to cope with your usual routine;
      • the 'normal' daytime rhythm shifting to the night, making you more alert and causing difficulty in getting to sleep.
      This can lead to

   • poor-quality sleep at night
   • feeling unwell
   • increased fatigue during the day
   • headaches

   • poor concentration, forgetfulness
   • low mood
   • muscle aches
   • loss of appetite
   • changes in bowel movements

7 **Concentration and memory problems**
   • Prolonged rest often means that people have less of a chance of having interesting things to occupy their minds. This lack of stimulation for the mind can cause concentration and memory problems.

8 **Vision and hearing changes**
   • Lying in bed for long periods of time results in body fluids moving towards your head. This may cause vision problems and sensitivity to noise.
   • When circadian rhythms are disrupted, it can affect the levels of cortisol (a hormone) in the body, which may in turn result in noise and light sensitivity.

This section highlighted some of the effects of increased rest and reduction in activities. So although it is natural to try to cope with fatigue by resting and reducing your activities, doing this can actually keep the fatigue going. The following diagram shows how.

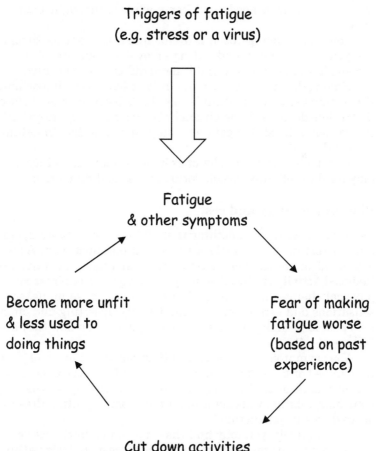

Triggers of fatigue
(e.g. stress or a virus)

Fatigue
& other symptoms

Become more unfit
& less used to
doing things

Fear of making
fatigue worse
(based on past
experience)

Cut down activities
that are tiring / stressful.

For people who are doing too much

Trying to do too much can put people at greater risk of developing CFS/ME. For some, this can sometimes simply be doing too much exercise. For others, it could be trying to do lots of different activities in the evenings and weekends on top of school/college and homework. Some may have a hobby that is very time-consuming. Others have a more complicated lifestyle because their parents are no longer living together and they stay with each parent at different times during the week. Other people may have a family member who has special needs or who is unwell, and that can take up extra time and energy.

Everyone is different, so even though you may know other people who seem to be doing just as much, it is important to be aware of your own needs and know what is the right balance for you.

Sometimes doing too much can make it seem as though everything is a chore and not as enjoyable anymore. You can become irritable and may find it more difficult to concentrate.

Having downtime for rest and relaxation is very important. If you think that your lifestyle may have been too busy before the fatigue developed, then it might be best not to aim to go back to that same lifestyle again and instead to aim for something more balanced.

If you are still doing a lot of exercise or many activities, you may need to set daily targets for more rest and relaxation.

Planning activity and rest

As discussed earlier, something that often keeps CFS/ME symptoms persisting is too little activity and too much rest. As we explained in the earlier section "Physical Effects of Rest and Reduced Activity', reduced activity and long periods of rest cause physical changes in the body. These changes cause unpleasant sensations and symptoms that can be very upsetting and often lead people to change their activities depending on how they are feeling.

Your symptoms may be so bad that you spend much of your time in bed or on a chair, and your days and nights can begin to run into each other. You may find that *any* activity – brushing your hair, talking, walking around the room or getting dressed or washed – is exhausting.

Alternatively, you may find that you can be fairly active on some days, but if you do too much you become more fatigued and your symptoms get worse, meaning that you can't do much on other days.

We all need rest to be healthy. People with CFS/ME often find that they rest more than they did in the past, but they rarely find it refreshing. This may be due to the following.

1 Your body does not get a chance to get used to a regular routine because you may be resting in response to your symptoms of fatigue and pain rather than in a planned way.
2 Although you probably *feel* that you need more rest, too much rest can be counterproductive; it may lead to disturbed sleep and reduced physical fitness and, in fact, can make you feel more tired. So although people usually think that if they're tired they need more rest, the opposite is often true – they actually need *more* activity or exercise!
3 It may be difficult for you to relax properly because you may find it hard to 'switch off' when you try to rest; for example, you may be thinking about how you are getting behind in your schoolwork.

If you always rest when you feel unwell, the symptoms will start to control you. CBT will help you control the chronic fatigue! If you have coped with fatigue by resting a lot, cutting down on your activities or only getting on with things when you feel well enough, it is more than likely that your body has lost its fitness.

Developing a regular activity programme

You probably have a number of things you would like to be able to do again. The aim of this part of CBT is to slowly help your body achieve fitness and greater stamina so that you can build up your activities and achieve these goals.

• The key to becoming more active is to make activity and rest **consistent**, regardless of how you feel. It is important that you plan small chunks of activity at regular intervals rather than long periods of occasional activity. As you increase your level of everyday activities you will gradually become stronger and will be able to cut down on rest.
• It is important to plan in advance what you are going to do on a regular daily basis by creating an **activity programme**. Try to plan to do about the same amount of activity and have the same number of rest periods each day. This may be

difficult for practical reasons, but aim to keep your routine as regular as possible.

Obviously the goals and targets you set for yourself will depend on how badly the CFS/ME affects you and what types of activities you would like to be able to do but cannot. Goals will be different for different people.

- **Keep targets realistic and achievable**

   For example, if you have not walked for a long time it would be better to set a target of walking for 10 minutes a day rather than walking for an hour.

- **Be specific about exactly what you would like to do**

   It is important that your target includes the following information:

1 The activity you want to do
2 How often you would like to carry out the activity
3 The length of time to be spent on the activity each time you do it

   Examples of specific targets include the following:

To have a friend over once a week for an hour
To walk every day for 10 minutes
To go to school for two hours each day
To spend five minutes each day tidying up
To help with cooking twice a week
To get up at 9:00am each day

What to include in your activity programme

It is important that you have *different* types of targets to work towards to make your life as balanced as possible. Enjoyable activities are as important as schoolwork. Here are some of the different types of goals that you may wish to include.

1 **Leisure time:** You may find that you have cut down on your previous hobbies or enjoyable activities, so you could think about which ones you would like to increase again.

2 **School or college:** If you are not going to school or college, or are not able to go for as many hours as you should, one of your targets could be to gradually increase the number of hours you spend at school.

3 **Seeing friends:** You may find that you have cut down on your time with friends or family or even lost contact with some. Consider a regular time for talking to or meeting up with those people. Or you may like to think about ways to meet new people.

4 **Exercise/sport:** You may want to think about a particular type of exercise or sport that you would like to take part in or work towards taking part in.

5 **Helping with chores:** You may have stopped helping with household chores (e.g. tidying your bedroom, helping with the cooking or washing up) and want to start doing some of these again.

6 **Sleep:** If sleep is a major problem, you may target a specific wake-up or bedtime.

Breaking down targets into steps

In order to reach your longer-term goals you will need to break them down into small steps. The steps should be tiny chunks of activity that you can practice often, if appropriate. Make the first step something you can easily do and make the next steps slightly harder each time.

Once you have been able to achieve the first step for a week or two, you may be able to move to the second step.

Here are some examples of longer-term targets that are broken down into easier steps.

Target 1: To get up at 9:30am

Steps towards Target 1:   Get up at 10:30am each day
Get up at 10:00am each day
Get up at 9:30am each day

Target 2: To walk 10 minutes twice a day, once in the morning and once in the afternoon

Steps towards Target 2:   Walk 2 minutes twice a day
Walk 5 minutes twice a day
Walk 7 minutes twice a day
Walk 10 minutes twice a day

Target 3: To study for 30 minutes in the morning and 30 minutes in the afternoon

Steps towards Target 3:   Study for 5 minutes in the morning and afternoon
Study for 10 minutes in the morning and afternoon
Study for 15 minutes in the morning and afternoon
Study for 20 minutes in the morning and afternoon
Study for 30 minutes in the morning and afternoon

After a couple of weeks, once you are in the habit of living in a more balanced way, you can add new activities to your routine.

Planning rest times

Resting is a time for you to try to *relax*. What you do in your rest time will depend on you as an individual. Some people find that reading is relaxing, others find it a major activity. Listening to music or the radio and watching television are other relaxing activities to consider. The important thing is that the rest time is used as a break from activity.

Try not to use your bed for resting or for sleeping during the day no matter how tired you feel. Sleeping in the day or resting in your room is likely to affect your sleep at night.

Starting your activity programme

Your symptoms may become slightly more severe when you start your programme. This happens because your body is getting used to the change in your usual routine. It does not indicate that you have harmed your body. Even though you may feel like resting more, it is important that you keep going with your activity programme. You will hopefully find that your symptoms will gradually decrease, although this may take a few weeks.

Remember: 'Hurt' does *not* equal 'harm'.

What to do on 'good' or 'bad' days

Do your best to stick to the plan regardless of whether you feel up to it. It's important that you don't do more than you planned if you feel good, but it is equally important to stick to your routine even when you feel unwell.

When should you reduce an activity target?

If you find after a couple of weeks that you have only been able to do a particular activity with about 25 per cent success or less, then you have probably set the activity level too high. You may need to reduce that activity for the next couple of weeks, although still keep it in your regular routine. For example, if your activity programme said that you should be reading for one hour a day, but you have only managed to do that for three days of the week and on the other days you haven't done any reading, then for the next couple of weeks it might be better to aim for only 30 minutes of reading each day.

Gradually increasing your activity levels

Once you have established a more regular pattern of activity and rest, you will then be able to start to *gradually* increase the amount of activity you do each day. This will probably be about two weeks after you start your programme, when you are more used to doing things at regular times. For example, if you have achieved a particular target (e.g. walking for 10 minutes each day) for most days during the previous week, it may be time to increase the target (e.g. increase the amount of time you spend walking each day to 15 minutes).

How often should you make changes to your activity programme?

How often you change your activity programme will depend on how successful you are in achieving your plans. However, we recommend that you spend 15–30 minutes each week reviewing your activity programme. This will give you the chance to assess your progress and help you to decide whether you can make any changes to your activity programme for the next week.

When should you introduce new activities?

You may consider introducing new activities:

- when you have achieved 75 per cent success overall with the activity programme from the previous week or fortnight.
- when you have achieved a target.
- if your rest periods have decreased and you have the time for more activities.
- if for circumstances beyond your control you are unable to continue a particular target.

To introduce a new activity refer to your target breakdown sheet and decide which target you would like to start working on. Introduce the first step towards achieving your target into your activity programme for the following week. When you have completed the first step in achieving your target, move on to the next step.

It is not necessary for your fatigue to have decreased for you to increase or start a new activity.

Rules for adding activities to your routine

Do very small chunks of the new activity spread throughout the day and week.

Start at a level that you can do easily. This will mean that you won't have a relapse of symptoms and fatigue when you begin to change your habits.

Don't do more or less than you planned. Even if you are having a bad day, stick to your plan and do at least as much as you did the day before. This will stop your body from losing the fitness that it has gained.

Don't worry if you notice that your symptoms increase when you start to follow the programme. You may feel dizzy, breathless and tired. It's usual to feel tired at first but this will fade. It doesn't mean that that the CBT isn't working or that the CFS/ME is getting worse. Your body is just getting used to it.

Don't give up! You may feel disheartened if the progress you are making is slow. But if you stick with it and make slow but steady progress you will gradually improve. Keep your old activity diaries and schedules to remind yourself how far you have come. The time it takes to recover your fitness is much longer than it took to lose the fitness. So be patient and persevere.

Eventually you'll reach your long-term goals!

How to decrease your rests

Once you have followed your programme for a few weeks you will have hopefully recovered from any temporary increase in fatigue and will feel that you are able to reduce your rests. Gradually cut down the amount of time you spend resting at first; then in a few weeks you may find that you can gradually reduce the number of rests.

Those who are severely affected

CFS/ME affects people to varying extents. Some are bed-bound, restricted to a wheelchair or not able to do very much activity. If CFS/ME affects you this severely, the activities that you begin with may be sitting up or getting out of bed for a few minutes, building up to standing for a few minutes or climbing a few stairs.

Those who are less affected by CFS/ME

You may be attending school full time but find yourself exhausted at the end of the day and have no energy on the weekends. Or there may be some aspects of your life that you don't have the energy for anymore, like playing a sport or keeping up a hobby. You may be living in a 'boom and bust' way, where on good days you achieve a lot and on bad days you only rest. If this describes you, you can also use the Weekly Activity Schedule provided earlier to balance your day and week with consistent rest and activity and gradually build in aspects of your life that you have neglected.

Keeping track of your progress

You can keep track of how well you are doing on the following Target Achievement Chart.

Here we provide an example of a completed Target Achievement Chart and then a blank one for you to photocopy.

In the left-hand column write down your activity targets for a particular week, and in the right-hand columns rate how well you stuck to your target for each day, if appropriate.

Difficulties you may encounter

Fear of making things worse

It is natural to be concerned about making things worse, particularly if you have had this experience in the past. When you start doing your activity programme, it is possible that your symptoms may increase. However, as long as you stick to a consistent amount of activity and rest, and only gradually increase your level of activity, any increase in symptoms should be only temporary. When you gradually increase your exercise levels, an increase in symptoms does not mean that you have harmed your body. It is usually a sign that your body is getting used to the new level of activity.

Target achievement chart

Example

Target	Monday	Tuesday	Wednesday	Thursday	Friday	Saturday	Sunday	Monday	Tuesday	Wednesday	Thursday	Friday	Saturday	Sunday
To get up by 9:00	✓	9:20	✓	✓	✓	9:45	9:30	✓	✓	✓	✓	9:15	9:40	9:10
To walk for five minutes in the morning	✓	✓	10 min	✓	✓	X	X	✓	✓	✓	✓	✓	20 min	✓
To walk for five minutes in the afternoon	X	✓	X	✓	✓	✓	✓	✓	X	✓	✓	X	X	✓
To read for 10 minutes in the morning	✓	✓	✓	✓	20 min	X	X	✓	✓	✓	✓	5 min	X	✓
To read for 10 minutes in the afternoon	✓	✓	✓	✓	✓	5 min	✓	✓	X	✓	✓	✓	X	X

(Continued)

Target achievement chart (Continued)

Example

Target	Monday	Tuesday	Wednesday	Thursday	Friday	Saturday	Sunday	Monday	Tuesday	Wednesday	Thursday	Friday	Saturday	Sunday
To text or phone a friend at least three times a week	X	Text Sam ✓	X	X	Phone Becky ✓	X	Phone Sam ✓	Text Jenni ✓	X	Text Jenni ✓	X	Text Sam ✓	X	Text Becky ✓
Comments						Felt very ill				Dad at home, helped with goals			Gran with us	

Target achievement chart

Target	Monday	Tuesday	Wednesday	Thursday	Friday	Saturday	Sunday	Monday	Tuesday	Wednesday	Thursday	Friday	Saturday	Sunday

Remember: 'Hurt' does *not* equal 'harm'.

Lack of motivation

Sometimes it can be very difficult to motivate yourself to work towards particular targets in your programme. For example, it can be difficult to force yourself to get out of bed at a set time when you don't have a particular reason to get up, like school. Lots of people find it hard to get up if they have nothing in particular to get up for. That is why it is important that your activity programme includes some targets that you can work towards and get a sense of achievement from. Getting up will then become easier.

If you have motivation problems with particular targets, you could get your parents to help. For example, they might be able to wake you up in the morning if you find it difficult to get up by just using an alarm clock.

To help motivate yourself sometimes it can help to plan a reward for when you are able to achieve difficult targets.

Doing too much on a good day

When you are having a good day it is very tempting to push yourself further and do more than usual. However, you are then putting yourself at risk of making your symptoms worse. It is therefore important to do roughly the same amount of activity every day, regardless of how you are feeling, and only build up the level of activity gradually. The idea of not doing more on a good day may be difficult to get used to, but once you have tried it a few times you should see that it makes you feel better in the long run.

Feeling down after a bad day

If you have a bad day it can be easy to get down and to start feeling pessimistic about getting better. However, this will only make it harder for you to keep going with your programme. Try to put the bad day behind you and carry on as usual. Setbacks and bad days are a normal part of recovery.

Putting yourself under pressure to get better quickly

When you have been feeling unwell for some time it is natural to want to get better right away. Unfortunately that isn't realistic in most cases – your body will need time to adjust to your activity programme and your new way of doing things. If things seem to be going slowly, try not to be hard on yourself because that will just add to your stress. Everyone recovers at a different rate. As long as you are keeping to a balance of activity and rest and gradually increasing your activity level, things should improve. Be proud of any progress you make, however small it may seem.

Having mixed feelings about getting better

When you have had CFS/ME for a while, it is common to have concerns about what it will be like when you get better. For example, you may worry about what it will be like to be back with your friends at school or to face exams again. There may have been parts of your life before you became unwell that were actually quite stressful.

These are natural concerns, and it may be helpful to talk to your parents or a friend about them. They may be able to help you think of ways to make it easier for you to return to 'normal' life. For example, if you were overdoing things before you developed CFS/ME, it does not make sense to simply return to that way of doing things. You will need to think about how to have a more balanced lifestyle that includes time for rest and relaxation. Having CFS/ME can be an opportunity to take a step back and think about what kinds of things you want to return to and which things you can leave behind. Sometimes this might mean cutting down on activities (e.g. the number of exams you will take), and sometimes it will mean changing your attitude towards them (e.g. putting less pressure on yourself to do things to a very high standard).

Having to deal with a virus or infection

Once you have started on your treatment programme, it can be extremely frustrating to become ill with a virus or something similar, especially if makes your CFS/ME symptoms worse. Illness can also cause worry about how much of your activity programme you should carry out.

If you have a cold you should try to carry on as usual. However, if you have a high temperature, you should rest for a while. If the virus has made you feel weak, you should cut out your sporting activities.

4

Dealing with unhelpful thoughts and attitudes

Most of the time, we don't pay much attention to the way we think. But it can have a strong impact on us. The way we think about a situation can make us feel better or worse. It can also affect what we do.

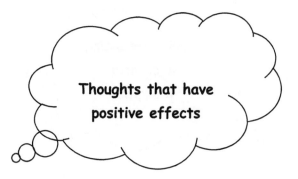

Thoughts that have positive effects

If we are looking forward to something – for example playing a new computer game – we have thoughts such as 'It's going to be really good; I can't wait'.

Thoughts like this help energise us to do things and make us feel motivated or excited. They help us get things done. Then after we've done the thing (played the new computer game), we carry on feeling good and have more positive thoughts because it was enjoyable.

So our thoughts affect our body (energising us), our feelings (making us excited) and our actions.

Everyone has negative thoughts too. They may happen more often when we're unwell, which is understandable. These thoughts can make us feel worse. They can make us feel more worried or low or drain our energy. In the following sections we will discuss how to identify and change these thoughts.

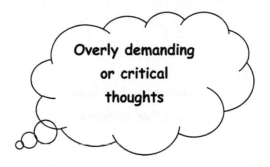

Imagine you have something coming up that is important to you, like a piece of coursework, a performance in a drama production or a sports event. Then think what it would be like if the teacher or team leader said, 'This is very difficult but unless you do it perfectly, there is no point in trying. Any mistakes mean that you've failed.' Unless you happened to be feeling super-confident that day, this might make you feel more worried about your performance beforehand. You may feel tempted to avoid it altogether. During the event you would probably be monitoring your performance for any mistakes, which might actually interfere with how well you perform. Afterwards you might keep going over the experience in your mind and feel unsatisfied with your performance, no matter how well you did.

Sometimes we talk to ourselves in that way without even noticing it. Although it is important to try hard and do well, if we are too harsh with ourselves, it can have a counterproductive effect and drain our motivation or self-esteem. Sometimes people say it's like having an evil gremlin or parrot on their shoulder saying critical things. If this affects you, see the next section, 'High Standards: When and How to Adjust'.

If you have been ill for quite a while, you can become disheartened and feel down. It can feel harder to do things. You could start to have negative thoughts, such as 'What's the point in trying to do more, I just feel worse' or 'I haven't seen my friends for so long they will have forgotten me'. Such thoughts can make you feel low and drain your energy and motivation even further. You may then be less likely to do anything, which makes you feel even worse. If you recognize this problem (we've all had it), see the section called 'Getting Back into the Habit of Enjoying Yourself'.

Imagine that if you are trying out a new computer game. Rather than looking forward to it, you are thinking, 'What if I can't concentrate well enough to be able to play it?' or 'What if playing it make me feel more exhausted?' Those thoughts would probably make you feel more anxious and discourage you from even trying the new game. Ways of testing out such thoughts are described in 'Testing out Anxious Predictions' and 'Problem-solving', both in chapter 5.

High standards: When and how to adjust

> ### Daniel
>
> Exams were looming for Daniel. Even though he had missed most of the last two terms of school, all his friends were doing the exams and he didn't want to be left behind. Not only that, he insisted that he would do all 11 exams and that he would get an A or A* in all of them. He thought that anything else would mean he had failed and let himself and his parents down. He tried to revise for exams on his own at home. He was able to do this for his two best subjects. But when he tried to do physics he found it difficult to understand, and he couldn't seem to learn the French vocabulary and grammar. He got more and more frustrated with his brain, which used to be so quick, whereas now it felt slow and easily confused. He became more anxious about the exams and kept trying harder and harder, but it only made him more and more exhausted. He felt overwhelmed and stressed out. His sleeping got even worse. In the end his parents decided it would be better if he didn't do any exams at all that year and he would take them next year instead. Daniel felt very disappointed but also a bit relieved that the pressure was over for now.

There is nothing wrong with aiming high. This can help people achieve more. What is different here is that Daniel's standards, what he expected of himself, were unrealistically high compared to his current abilities. If he hadn't also been trying to recover from CFS/ME, maybe these standards would have been more reasonable. Perhaps when he was well Daniel was the kind of person who excelled fairly easily in academic things and thus expecting a lot of As and A*s was reasonable.

Or maybe not. Perhaps Daniel had always expected too much of himself, thinking that only an A was good enough. Maybe he had always pushed himself too hard, which might have made him vulnerable to illness. In the next section we will look at this in more detail. Hopefully you will get a good idea of how to tackle some of the more unhelpful ways of thinking. This is a skill that would be useful for everyone to learn.

Where do high standards come from?

It doesn't really matter where the high standards come from. The key thing is to make sure that unrealistic standards are not getting in the way of your recovery. However, some people find it helpful to think about where they got their high standards. Here are three common sources.

Yourself

For some people, how well they perform in exams or in other situations is a very important factor in how they feel about themselves. Maybe you are the kind of person for whom a B has never felt good enough. Or maybe you worry about what other people would think of you if you didn't always perform to a high standard. There is some evidence that people with this kind of perfectionism are more likely to get fatigued.

Your family

It could be that you come from a family of high achievers. You might be trying to keep up with brothers or sisters or parents who have always achieved excellent results, even if you have a different set of strengths or abilities.

Or maybe you've done well in the past and the praise from your family felt really good, so you want to keep it up. Often there is no direct pressure on you to achieve high results, and no one would want you to wear yourself out trying to overachieve. It's just a habit you have developed.

People at school

Maybe you have done well in the past and feel that teachers or classmates expect you to get high marks the time. Teachers are often under a lot of stress to produce good results in their class, which can translate into pressure on their students. Some schools or teachers are more pressured than others.

Regardless of where this pressure comes from – you, your family or your school – it doesn't mean it's necessarily bad. However, it is not *useful at the moment*. So what you can do about it?

Pros and cons of high standards

Let's go back to Daniel. A useful way to start tackling your problems in this area is to look at the advantages and the disadvantages of high standards.

Consider Daniel's chart:

Very high standards

Advantages	Disadvantages
Sense of achievement if I can meet the high standards.	Get stressed out before exams.
Aiming high helped me keep motivated and work hard, and in the past that hadn't caused a problem.	Feel bad about myself if don't get the grade I want.
	Spending so much time on schoolwork and revision gets in the way of other things I want to do.
	I get tired from working so hard.
	I just couldn't keep up with the high standards all the time.
	Sometimes I feel under so much pressure I put off starting my work.

So the disadvantages were outweighing the benefits. Daniel has set his standards so high that he could not possibly meet them. They had become counterproductive and self-defeating. His high standards meant that he actually achieved nothing!

The paradox: By adjusting (unreasonably high) standards we achieve more.

You might want to try using this type of table to write the disadvantages and advantages of having high standards for yourself. See if you can come up with more advantages and disadvantages than Daniel.

Why lowering standards is not as stupid as it sounds

'Lowering' standards is actually a misleading phrase. Actually it is about *prioritising* where to place your attention and energy.

One of Daniel's problems was that he wanted to do well in *all* subjects, even those he had never really liked or those that were not suited to his abilities. For most of us, this is completely unrealistic. Many of us have one or two subjects that we really like and succeed in. Then there is a bigger number that we are just okay at. There might be one or two or maybe a few that we struggle with. It's reasonable to want to do well in the ones you are good at. It is completely unrealistic to expect A*s in the ones that you struggle with.

What could Daniel have done differently? Prioritised. In any set of things to be achieved there are some that are more important than others. Let's look at the following Prioritising Chart.

How to use the Prioritising Chart

The Prioritising Chart can be used when you realise you've got too much going on or when you are feeling overwhelmed. First make a list of your current activities, both exams and other stuff – sports, hobbies, social activities and so on. Then rate how important the activities are for you. Keep two things in mind – how much you need them for your 'next step' and other benefits such as enjoyment.

Looking at Daniel's chart, you can see that he wasn't sure what he wanted to do after he finishes school, but he thought it might involve Design and Technology or Geography. This gave him an idea of subjects that he needed. Next he thought about the subjects that he liked, even though he didn't need them. The ones that he neither liked nor needed got the lowest marks.

Looking at his list, Daniel then decided which subjects he would focus on and which he could worry about a bit less. This made him feel less pressured. He chose to drop some subjects and activities, at least for now. Some of these he would have to negotiate with his school.

Having unreasonably high expectations is like having a particularly nasty gremlin on your shoulder saying that you could always be doing better and that other people will think badly of you if you make a mistake or get anything less than a high mark. This makes you feel more anxious and tense so you can't perform as well. If the gremlin isn't there you can perform better because you're more relaxed. High standards are like gremlins or an inner critic in our brains – nothing is ever good

Prioritising chart

Example

Things to do	Importance (0–10) and why	I will prioritise . . .	I'll focus less on . . .	I'll drop . . . until . . .
Academic:		English, History, Geography and Maths.	I'll focus less on languages, particularly German as I don't even like it. Same with the sciences, particularly the physics, which I missed most of this year in. I'll worry less about dance; if I miss some weeks that's fine.	I'll see if I can drop Religious Studies and English Literature. I might also ask about the German and the biology; if I don't have to do them I don't see the point. Will drop swimming because it's too much right now and I'm bored with it. I might start again in September. Same with dance class.
History	7 – want to do A level			
Geography	8 – want to do A level			
Maths	8 – need it	I'll focus first on the English because I'm furthest behind with that.		
Physics	3 – don't like or need			
Biology	3 – don't like or need			
Art	5 – quite like it	I'll get my art up-to-date because that is fun and will be a good break from the other subjects.		
Religious Studies	2 – don't like or need			
French	4 – it's ok			
German	2 – don't like or need			
English	8 – need it	I only need to get above C in five subjects so I'll focus on these ones.		
English Lit.	2 – don't like or need			
Design and Tech.	8 – want to do A level			
Other:				
Swimming	0 – don't like it now			
Band practice	4 – fun	I'll keep up the babysitting because it's easy and I need the money and the band practice because it's fun.		
Dance class	2 – not bothered			
Babysitting	7 – money!			

Prioritising chart

Things to do	Importance (0–10) and why	I will prioritise . . .	I'll focus less on . . .	I'll drop . . . until . . .

enough for them, so they make us feel bad about ourselves and actually make us perform worse. Are you feeling overwhelmed? Try using this technique. Tell your inner critic or gremlin that they can say what they want but you're not going to buy into what they're saying anymore. You know that they can say only critical things, but that doesn't make those things true. Maybe imagine the gremlin's voice getting quieter and quieter so it's easier to ignore. Or maybe picture pushing the gremlin off your shoulder! You'll feel much better afterwards.

All-or-nothing thinking

The inner critic or gremlin may say that unless something is perfect, an A, it's not worth anything. You are told that there is no point doing something if you get an average grade or doing it just because you enjoy it. Unless you can be the best at your chosen sport, or be in the popular crowd at school or have a lead part in the play, you've failed, so don't even bother. If you can't concentrate 100 per cent of the time and or if you can't remember everything after you've read it the first time, that voice calls you stupid.

This happens often to people who have been very good at things. There was a boy in our clinic who used to be able to swim 40 lengths of a pool quite quickly. Part of his programme for getting better was to start swimming again . . . but differently this time. Obviously he couldn't go back to 40 fast lengths, which would just wear him out straight away. We suggested he start with five slow lengths.

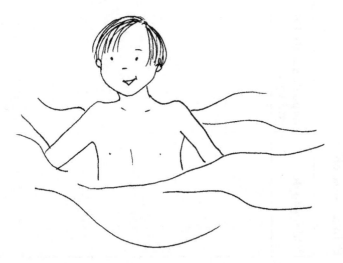

The boy responded (in a disgusted voice), 'Five slow lengths! But that's just piddling about – I'm not doing that, it's pointless.' With some persuasion he did try five. He found even that tiring and ended up doing three for a while. Then five became easier. Then seven, and so on. His inner critic had told him that it was 40 fast lengths or nothing, just like yours might be telling you it's A*s or failure or remembering everything the first time you read it or being completely stupid. Our boy was eventually able to do 40 fast lengths again, but he needed to 'piddle about' for a time first.

The way to shut up your inner critic or gremlin is to go back to the page on 'Breaking Down Targets Into Steps' in chapter 3. Between 0 and 40, there are lots of little steps to be walked (or swum). Map them out and take credit for each one you manage, not just the end goal. Combined with your focusing list, you might decide that 20 is good enough, or a C is good enough or going to the cinema rather than to the club is fine. Remember it's only the nasty inner critics or gremlins who think that nothing less than perfect is good enough.

'There's no point trying': Getting stuck

Our thoughts can make things worse for us in other ways too. They can keep us from doing things that would actually make us feel better – see the following example.

Alesha

It had been weeks since Alesha had left the house. Sometimes her mum would try to encourage her to come to the shops just a few minutes away: 'It'll do you good.' But Alesha would have thoughts like 'There's no point. The shops are stupid and tiring and I might bump into school friends and there is no way I'm ready for that.' 'Why don't you help me make a cake, you used to love baking,' tried Mum. Alesha would think, 'I don't like baking any more, nothing is enjoyable now I'm ill.' Mum would try again: 'Why don't you see if Chantell could come over, you two always have a laugh.' Alesha thought, 'I don't feel like laughing and I would just bring Chantell down. She's probably sick of me already and I don't want to risk losing her as a friend.' Alesha decided that maybe if she felt better she would try her mum's suggestions, but not right now. She'd wait until she had more energy and motivation.

Most of us have felt like this at one time or another. With long-lasting fatigue it is particularly easy to get a bit stuck. Our enthusiasm for things can drain away. It can feel as though something has taken the wind out of our sails. If we are lucky, something will come along and help us move along. More often than not though, we need to row our way out, at least at first.

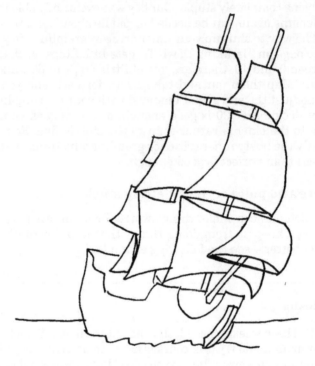

What keeps us stuck?

So what keeps us stuck? Let's consider Alesha. Before you read any further, you might want to think about some of the things affecting Alesha's feelings. Here are some hints: there are some things that are related to her circumstances, there are others relate to how she is thinking and there are still others that have to do with what she is (or is not) doing.

It's understandable that Alesha's circumstances are a bit depressing. She is on her own at home with CFS/ME and everyone she knows is at school. It feels as though there is nothing she can do, but is that true? Maybe there is not much she can do to see big improvements in her situation immediately, but she could change things a little bit; she could row to where there is a little more wind. What is stopping her is partly how she is thinking.

Alesha's mind is coming up with a lot of negative predictions. Everything that her mum suggests, Alesha predicts will be boring or tiring or pointless, and that it won't change anything. So she doesn't do it and so . . . nothing changes. She is also mind reading, assuming that she knows exactly what her friend Chantell is thinking and how she will react to her. So she doesn't see her friend and Alesha continues to feel low and lonely and worried what Chantell thinks of her.

Like many people who get stuck, Alesha has become so bored, listless and depressed that she has lost the energy and motivation to do much at all. By waiting for the tide to turn by itself, waiting for her motivation to return before trying anything, she has become stuck in a vicious circle. The less she does the worse she feels and the worse she feels the less she does. This is a horrible place to be. However, there are some things that she can do to break out of the vicious circle.

Getting unstuck

The most important thing is to stop waiting for energy or motivation to return before making changes. Many people think that you should wait until you feel *motivated*, until you feel like doing something, before you do it. However, we can help to rebuild our sense of motivation or drive by starting to do things again *before* we really feel like it. We need to *do* it first, *and then* over time we begin to *feel* like doing it. This is how things can begin to change and get unstuck.

So how could Alesha start getting unstuck? First she could look at her negative predictions. Take a look at the following Getting Unstuck Chart.

Alesha decided to call Chantell. Although it was just as tiring as she thought it would be, it was much more enjoyable. It also helped her realise that Chantell was a good friend and would stick by her even though Alesha wasn't at school at the moment. This made Alesha feel a bit better about her situation.

This experience also helped Alesha feel a little more open to the idea that she could do things that would change her mood.

Feeling better about yourself

When we stop doing things, we lose opportunities to feel a sense of achievement. When we decide to do something and then do it, we naturally feel pleased with ourselves because we have

Things I could do to change the way I feel	How enjoyable or tiring I predict they will be (0–10)	Action plan for testing out my predictions Reason for plan	How was it? Enjoyable, tiring? Re-rate
Bake a cake	Tiring 7 Enjoyable 3	I'll try calling Chantell and see if she wants to watch TV with me for a couple of hours. It *might* cheer me up.	We chatted a lot as well as watching TV. I was tired afterwards (4) but I really enjoyed it (8). Chantell seemed to enjoy it too.
Call Chantell	Tiring 4 Enjoyable 4		
Go to the shops with Mum	Tiring 8 Enjoyable 2		

carried out our plan. This can come from things that might seem small – making a phone call you have been putting off, doing a piece of school coursework, tidying your room or reading a section of this book.

These activities are not necessarily enjoyable, but they do lead to feeling better about yourself and to a sense that you have achieved something. When we have very little energy, it is easy to lose sight of the fact that even little achievements matter. In fact small achievements are even more important at this time. Our gremlin or inner critic may be telling us we should be able to do everything. This is an example of the all-or-nothing thinking mentioned earlier. Setting little goals for ourselves and achieving them helps us gain the courage and energy to work towards the bigger ones.

Let us rewrite the Getting Unstuck Chart to include a sense of achievement and see what else Alesha did.

Getting back into the habit of enjoying yourself

When we are well, enjoying things just happens naturally. However, when we get stuck we are out of practice at enjoying ourselves. We are in a rut and it can take practice to get back into enjoying the things that we used to. It's important to write your own list of things that you used to enjoy because no one else can really know exactly what it feels like for you, even though they might make helpful suggestions. Next pick one of the things on your list – one of the easier ones – and start practising. It may feel strange at first but most people find that it's easier than they expected once they've gotten started. They had often forgotten how and why they had enjoyed those activities, but with a little practice the enjoyment begins to come back.

Things I could do to change the way I feel	How enjoyable or tiring or how much of a sense of achievement I predict (0–10)	Action plan for testing out my predictions Reason for plan	How was it? Enjoyable, tiring, feeling of achievement? Re-rate
Bake a cake	Tiring 7 Enjoyable 3 Achievement 5	Go to the shops with Mum. Walking will build my strength and will help improve my confidence too. It might be nice to get outdoors.	Less tiring (5) and more enjoyable (4) than I expected. I got a new magazine. More importantly, I feel I've done something to help myself get better. Mum was pleased too. (8)
Call Chantell	Tiring 4 Enjoyable 4 Achievement 2		
Go to the shops with Mum	Tiring 8 Enjoyable 2 Achievement 5		

It's not about positive thinking

We have seen in previous sections that particular thoughts and ways of thinking can either (a) make us feel bad (anxious, low, frustrated, etc.) or (b) lead to us to behave in unhelpful ways (e.g. avoiding doing things we should be doing or pushing ourselves too hard). It is often possible to find more helpful and realistic alternatives to your unhelpful thoughts. By coming up with helpful and realistic alternatives, our negative feelings often recede a bit. It can be helpful to complete a Balanced Thinking Record like the ones on the following pages.

How to complete the chart

Situation column

- Write what you were doing or thinking about when you noticed having a strong feeling or change in your mood.

Feeling column

- Note the feeling or emotion (e.g. anxious, sad, frustrated, irritated, guilty, embarrassed, annoyed, scared or low) you felt at the time that you had your unhelpful thought.
- Rate the strength of your feeling on a 0–100 per cent scale, with 100 being the most strongly you have ever had that feeling.

Unhelpful thought column

- Write the actual thought(s) that went through your mind.
- It is most helpful to write a sentence summarising the meaning of the thought (e.g. 'I'm never going to get this finished in time') rather than simply an exclamation such as 'oh no'.
- Write down how much you believe each thought on a 0–100 per cent scale.

Alternative thoughts column

- The alternative thoughts column is the most important but also the most difficult. It is where you try to find a different way of looking at the situation based on all the available evidence.
- The alternative thought is often more positive than the initial thought but it is *not* merely switching a positive thought for a

negative thought. Positive thinking tends to ignore negative information and can be as unhelpful as negative thinking.
- We are aiming for balanced thinking that takes into account all of the information, both negative and positive.

Here are some questions that you can ask yourself to help get a different perspective on the situation.

Tips for coming up with alternative, balanced ways of thinking

1 If a friend was in a similar situation, what might I say to them?
2 If someone who is close to me knew I was thinking these things, what would they say to me?
3 Am I making a thinking error (e.g. all-or-nothing thinking, making negative predictions or mind reading)?
4 Is this type of thinking going to lead me to avoid things that would be helpful to do, or will it encourage me to push myself too hard and make me feel worse?
5 What is the actual evidence that this thought is true?
6 Is there any evidence that this thought may not be entirely accurate?
7 Am I being too self-critical and expecting too much of myself?
8 If I continue to think in this way, is it going to have negative effects (e.g. keep me feeling low, stop me from doing things, make me irritable, etc.)?
9 What are the advantages and disadvantages of thinking this way?

Outcome column

- Re-rate the intensity of your feelings on a 0–100 per cent scale. We cannot expect that this technique will make negative feelings disappear entirely, but it can sometimes help reduce them so you are more in control.

Action plan column

- Write down any ways that will help you feel better or deal with the situation. This can help you move forward rather than continue to dwell on things.

Dealing with unhelpful thoughts: Summary

Thoughts can have a very powerful effect on a person. They can make a good situation bad or a bad situation worse. However, they are only thoughts – passing events in the mind – *they are not facts*. Even if they seem plausible, it does not mean they are true. This section has given you some ideas about how to take a step back from your thoughts and feelings, as well as some ways of testing out just how true those thoughts are.

We have seen that certain types of thinking can make things worse:

- All-or-nothing thinking ('it's got to be an A* or it's worthless') and high standards make the things we have to do more difficult, turning molehills into mountains.
- Anxious predictions (also sometimes called catastrophic thoughts) make us feel that we will not be able to cope with whatever we have to do. See the section in chapter 5, 'Testing Out Anxious Predictions', for more about anxious predictions.
- Pessimistic thoughts and predictions (there's no point, I won't enjoy it anyway') leaving us feeling low, hopeless and a bit stuck.

To change the way we way we think:

1 We can identify the unhelpful thought and how it makes us feel. We can also check out the type of thought: Was it an anxious prediction or a bit all or nothing?
2 We can test this thought out either by trying out what we thought was going to be so bad or by looking at the evidence for the thought.

Thoughts can be powerful, but that doesn't mean they have to dictate our feelings completely. By using some of these techniques, you can take more control over what you do. This is one part of the process of feeling better.

How avoidance makes molehills into mountains

The single most unhelpful thing that we do can be summed up in a simple word: AVOID.

When we find a situation difficult, it is understandable that we are tempted to avoid it, because in the short term that means bypassing the difficult feelings associated with it. However, we pay the price with the long-term consequences. The more we avoid dealing with it, the more difficult it becomes.

Balanced thinking record

Example

Situation	Unhelpful thoughts	Emotion (rate intensity: 0–100%)	Alternative response (balanced thinking)	Outcome (re-rate moods now)	Action plan (what can you do now?)
Walking to shop	My legs hurt and feel weak. Maybe I'm making myself worse.	Worried 80%	It is to be expected that my legs will feel tired and hurt; my muscles will have lost much less exercise lately. I might feel a bit worse in the short term but if I keep on gradually building up my exercise, my body will get stronger again and feel better eventually.	Worried 30%	Relax by surfing the Internet when I'm back home again. Don't dwell on the pain. Remind myself that the pain and strange feelings after exercise are signs that I am building up my muscle strength; it doesn't mean I have damaged myself.

Balanced thinking record

Example

Situation	Unhelpful thoughts	Emotion (rate intensity: 0–100%)	Alternative response (balanced thinking)	Outcome (re-rate moods now)	Action plan (what can you do now?)
Hearing that my school friends have been doing lots of fun and interesting things	Everyone is getting on with their lives and forgetting me. I'm getting left out. No one will want to be friends with me when I go back to school.	Down 80% Anxious 50%	It's to be expected that I'm not as involved with everyone as I used to be because I'm not often at school. But Freya and Simon still phone me and keep me up-to-date. There is no reason why I can't get back into things again when I'm feeling better. Maybe I need to make a bit more of an effort to keep in touch with people. I can't leave it all to them.	Down 40% Anxious 20%	Phone Tom. I haven't spoken to him in ages. Ask Jo if she wants to come round after school one day.

Balanced thinking record

Situation	Unhelpful thoughts	Emotion (rate intensity: 0–100%)	Alternative response (balanced Thinking)	Outcome (re-rate moods now)	Action plan (what can you do now?)

The more difficult it becomes, the more we are likely to avoid it, and so on. A vicious circle develops. This applies to a lot of situations relating to stress and fatigue. For example, you may feel overwhelmed by the amount of homework you have to do, particularly if you are already fatigued and finding it difficult to concentrate. So you decide to leave it for the night. The next day you get more. You feel even more tired and overwhelmed at the thought of it. You leave it for another night; the next day you get even more homework. This is how molehills become mountains.

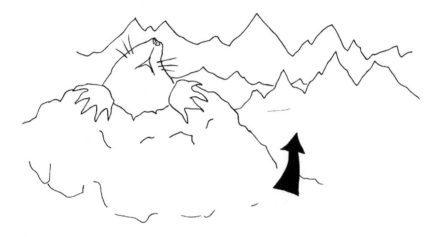

This can happen surprisingly quickly. The longer this cycle goes on, the more anxious and low we become. (It can also make you feel worse physically, as discussed elsewhere in this book.) The worse we feel, the more likely it is that we will avoid even more. So what's the answer? *Just do it.* If you *can* just do it, it works. However, that can be easier said than done. If you've been avoiding something for a long time, it's not so simple. You need to start doing it again gradually and systematically. Chapter 5, 'Dealing with Stress and Anxiety', explains more and gives suggestions about how to do this. Directly facing what you have avoided creates the opposite of a vicious circle: the more you do something you've been avoiding, the easier it gets and the better you feel.

5

Dealing with stress and anxiety

The stress response

We all feel stressed or anxious from time to time. Anxiety can help us react to a stressful situation. It can help us think and act quickly in situations such as exams or interviews or those in which we are in danger. Feeling anxious is part of our normal behaviour.

The symptoms of stress and anxiety can be mild, as when we just feel tense or 'wound up'. They can also be severe, as when we experience feelings of dread, fear or panic.

Having CFS/ME can be very stressful at times. Not only do you have to deal with the symptoms, but you may also have other concerns, such as not being able to do your schoolwork properly or not doing things with your friends as much as you used to. These things may at times make you feel worried or anxious.

You may find that you have uncomfortable feelings of anxiety when you have to do something new or something that you haven't done for a long time. You may be lacking confidence because you are out of practice. The feelings of anxiety may be making it hard for you to do things you really want to.

Understanding how anxiety affects our body, our thoughts and our behaviour helps us cope with it.

The effects of stress and anxiety on the body

Stress and anxiety can lead to many different symptoms in the body. The following image shows common signs of extreme stress and anxiety.

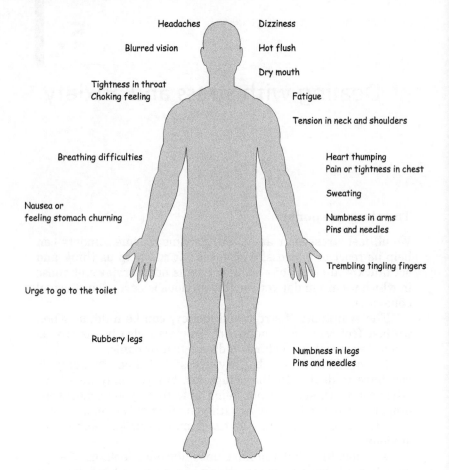

Headaches
Dizziness
Blurred vision
Hot flush
Dry mouth
Tightness in throat
Choking feeling
Fatigue
Tension in neck and shoulders
Breathing difficulties
Heart thumping
Pain or tightness in chest
Sweating
Nausea or
feeling stomach churning
Numbness in arms
Pins and needles
Trembling tingling fingers
Urge to go to the toilet
Rubbery legs
Numbness in legs
Pins and needles

These physical symptoms can be very uncomfortable and distressing. It is easy to think that there is something seriously wrong, but it is important to remember that these symptoms cannot harm you. They are the body's normal reaction to stress.

How stress and anxiety can cause physical symptoms

When we feel stressed or anxious, physical changes occur in our body, partly as a result of an increased amount of the hormone adrenaline being released into the bloodstream. These natural changes have a protective function, preparing us for action when we feel threatened or encounter a stressful situation. However, the physical feelings that we experience during times of anxiety can be very unpleasant.

Everyone experiences physical symptoms of anxiety in a different way, but here are some of the most common symptoms:

1 **Increased heart rate**

This can cause a racing pulse, palpitations and pounding or tightness in the chest. Some people feel very frightened by these sensations and can become more anxious, resulting in a further release of adrenaline that keeps the physical sensations going.

2 **Altered blood flow**

When a person is anxious, blood is redirected to the major muscle groups to prepare for action. This may cause pale skin, pain, cold hands and feet and sometimes numbness or tingling. Reduced blood flow to the bowel affects the passage of food and can result in diarrhoea, constipation or discomfort in the abdomen.

3 **Muscle tension**

There is an increase in muscle tension to prepare them for action. This can cause aches, pain (particularly in the shoulders, neck, jaws and head) and fatigue. Twitching or trembling muscles may also occur.

4 **Sweating**

In order to cool the body down, sweating increases, which can cause clammy hands and feet.

5 **Visual changes**

The visual system changes, for example by allowing the eye to let in more light and by changing the shape of the eye lens to improve side and distance vision. These changes can be experienced as blurring of vision.

6 **Breathlessness, which can lead to hyperventilation**

A natural response to feeling stressed is for overbreathing to occur, to fill the lungs with oxygen and prepare us for action. If overbreathing continues for a while it is called hyperventilation. This can cause a variety of unpleasant symptoms:

- Light-headedness, dizziness, faintness, feeling unsteady, clumsiness, blurred vision, pins and needles, tingling or numbness (sometimes one-sided) in the limbs or face, cramp-like muscle spasms (particularly in the hands and feet), increased sensitivity to light and noise, feelings of being detached from oneself, feelings of unreality or a sense of being out of control.

  These symptoms occur because hyperventilation reduces the amount of carbon dioxide in the blood. This changes the balance of chemicals in the blood, causing tightening of the blood vessels and reduced blood supply, especially in the brain. Although you may feel faint, this does not mean that fainting will actually occur. This is because overall blood pressure is high in anxiety and fainting only occurs when blood pressure is very low.

- Chest pain or discomfort. This is because hyperventilation can cause the muscles of the chest wall to be overused.
- Headaches and pain/stiffness in the neck and shoulders. These can occur because overbreathing results in increased use of muscles in the head, neck and shoulders.
- Dry mouth and throat, swallowing difficulties, tightness in the throat and the feeling of having a lump in the throat. These can occur because of overuse of neck muscles in hyperventilation or excessive mouth breathing and reduced saliva production when anxious.

7 **Weakness and exhaustion**
The bodily changes that occur when you are anxious (e.g. increased adrenaline levels and activity of the nerves) can cause feelings of weakness and exhaustion that add to the fatigue and muscle aches of CFS/ME.

8 **Sleep disturbance**
The adrenaline released at times of stress can cause sleep disturbance, nightmares and night sweats.

9 **Mental functioning**
Anxiety may affect mental functioning in a number of ways and contribute to the following:
- Mood changes (e.g. irritability, being easily upset)
- Concentration problems, forgetfulness, decision-making difficulties
- Restlessness (e.g. fidgety, can't sit still)
- Tendency to go over things again and again.

10 **Flu-like symptoms**
During extreme or long-lasting mental effort or physical exercise, there is increased activity of the nervous system and adrenaline production. This can lead to overwhelming symptoms including aches and pains, headache, sweating, feeling hot and cold, chest tightness and sore throat. These are similar to the symptoms of a flu-like illness. They can make a person think that they are coming down

with a virus and cause them to rest more often, which can lead to further deconditioning or unfitness.

11 **Panic attacks**

Extreme anxiety symptoms can be very unpleasant but are not dangerous. However, the person can easily mistake them for signs of a serious disease or think that something terrible is about to happen (e.g. that they are going to die, collapse or lose control). This makes them more anxious, which can trigger further unpleasant symptoms, and this cycle can occasionally end up turning into a panic attack.

The vicious circle of anxiety

As well as causing bodily symptoms, anxiety is also associated with changes in our thinking and behaviour. These effects on our body, thinking and behaviour are linked and can fuel each other. This means that we can become caught in a vicious circle of anxiety that is hard to break out of.

Body:

We experience distressing bodily **symptoms**, e.g. headaches, dizziness, fatigue, blurred vision.

Thoughts:

We tend to **worry** and have unhelpful thoughts, such as 'I can't cope' and 'I'm not ready for this'. We may think there is something seriously wrong as we experience bodily symptoms of anxiety.

Behaviour:

We may **avoid** certain situations because they make us feel anxious. This can make us even more anxious when we have to face the situation again, as we are not used to dealing with it.

Sami

Sami thought that if she met up with a group of friends, she wouldn't be able to talk and joke in the same way that she used to. This thought led to her being anxious about going out with them, which in turn resulted in symptoms such as a racing heart, a headache and feeling shaky and tense. These symptoms made it harder to concentrate on the conversation, which fuelled her fears that she wouldn't be able to talk normally. So the anxious thoughts and symptoms fed into each other. Afterwards she decided that she wasn't well enough to be going out, and she tried to avoid it in the future. This prevented her from learning how to deal with these situations, so next time when she did try to go the anxiety was still there.

Common worries of people with CFS/ME

If you have been ill for a long time, it is likely that your lifestyle has changed and you have stopped doing a lot of the things you used to do. As you get better, although you may feel good about starting these activities again, you may worry about them, thinking, for example, 'Will I be able to cope?'

These worries are normal quite simply because if we don't do something regularly we lose confidence in our ability to do it.

Following are some of the worries that patients often describe:

- going back to school
- catching up with missed work
- coping with schoolwork
- starting new studies
- catching up with friends
- playing sports
- taking up activities again
- becoming ill again
- not knowing what to tell friends about their illness

For some people these worries can be so severe that they can cause them to stop doing something they really want to do. The next section is about dealing with your worries and describes two different ways to do this: testing out anxious predictions and problem-solving.

Testing out anxious predictions

When you have CFS/ME it is easy to get out of practice doing certain things. When you don't practice things regularly you may lose confidence in yourself. This can be true even for things such as seeing your friends or going to the shops, which you wouldn't have thought twice about before you developed these symptoms.

You may have some specific concerns about what would happen if you were in a certain situation. For example, you might think 'If I go into the supermarket I will get dizzy and might pass out' or 'If I try phoning Freya she will be too busy to talk to me'. We call these kinds of thoughts 'anxious predictions'.

One way to help yourself overcome anxiety is to practice going into feared situations to test out whether your anxious prediction was accurate. You may learn that the thing you feared doesn't actually happen, or if it does, you can find ways to cope with the fear.

Here are some guidelines:

1 **Write a list of all the situations that cause you anxiety.**
Write them in order from the least difficult to the most difficult and start with the easiest thing on your list.
2 **Be clear and specific about what you are going to do.**
E.g. phone a particular friend at 7:00pm.
3 **Practice regularly and as frequently as possible.**
This obviously depends on the type of situation that makes you feel anxious. Some situations are easier to practice with regularity than others. Examples might be phoning a friend for 15 minutes three times a week or going into a crowded shop for at least 10 minutes twice a week.
4 **Stay in the situation until your anxiety lessens.**
Although feeling anxious is uncomfortable, it is not harmful. Do not leave the situation until your anxiety subsides and you feel a little better.
5 **Expect to feel anxious.**
If you haven't been in certain situations for a while, it is normal to feel anxious. Wait and give the feelings of anxiety time to pass. The symptoms are not pleasant but they cannot harm you!
6 **Use the Testing out Anxious Predictions form.**
This will help you learn more about what is driving your fear of the particular situation, whether your fears are realistic and whether there are ways of coping if your feared outcome does occur.

Following is an example of a completed form.

Situation	Anxious prediction What are your fears about this situation?	Result of practice Did the things you feared happen? If so, how did you cope? What you have learnt from this practice?
Phoning Paul	My voice will go strange. I will stumble over my words. He will think I'm stupid.	I did stumble over a few words when I first started speaking, but as soon as the conversation got going it was fine. He didn't seem to think I was stupid. I learnt that even if I do stutter or say things wrong, it passes quickly. People don't seem to notice as much as I think they will.

When you have tested out your anxious prediction by going into the feared situation and using this form, this should help you to:

1 Change your predictions if they turned out to be untrue. (For example, the new prediction might be 'I may stumble over my words at first but it will pass quickly and not be a problem').
   or
2 Plan ways to cope if the fears turn out to be true. (For example, if you continue to stutter and stumble over words throughout a conversation, you could think about whether to ignore it if the other person doesn't seem to mind, or to talk to your friend about it to see if he notices or to get more practice at talking on the phone to see if that helps to reduce it.) The 'Problem-solving' section that follows may help you with these plans.

Testing out Anxious Predictions Form

Date	Situation	Anxious prediction What are your worst fears about this situation?	Result of practice Did your worst fears happen? If so, how did you cope? What you have learnt from this practice?

Problem-solving

Problem-solving techniques can also help you deal with your worries. First make a list of any situations or activities that worry you. Decide what you want to tackle first. It might be better to tackle the things that you are least worried about first. As you become more confident you can tackle the more worrying situations. The following box describes how to solve problems in steps.

Problem-solving

1 What is your problem?
   Clearly write down exactly what your problem is.
2 Think of at least three different ways to solve the problem.
   Try to see the problem from the point of view of someone you think is good at solving problems or has dealt with similar problems in the past: 'If _____ was in my shoes what would he/she do?'
3 Write down what you think the result of each of your solutions might be.
4 Decide which solution you think would give the best result.
5 Make a plan and carry out that solution.
6 Did your solution work?

This chapter includes an example of how this can be done, as well as a blank form where you can write down your own problem-solving.

This way of solving problems may seem long and boring, but once you have done this a few times you may find that you can solve problems in your head without having to write them down. Make some time to tackle your worries in this way in your Activity Programme.

PROBLEM-SOLVING SHEET

EXAMPLE

MY PROBLEM: *My coursework needs to be in by the end of the week and there's no way I'll get it done.*

ALTERNATIVE SOLUTIONS (Think of at least 3)

1 *I could just forget about it and give up.*

2 *I could stay up all night and work really hard.*

3 *I could just hand it in late.*

4 *I could ask for an extension.*

EVALUATE SOLUTIONS (What is a possible result of each solution?)

1 *I'll feel down. I may have to start the subject over again.*

2 *I'll be exhausted for ages. That might set me back with other work.*

3 *It might not be accepted.*

4 *They're very strict about that sort of thing. They might say no — that teacher doesn't have much sympathy.*

THE BEST SOLUTION IS NUMBER *4*

MY PLAN TO CARRY OUT THE SOLUTION

I'll ask the teacher who knows the most about my illness about the policy for extensions and see if that teacher will speak to my teacher about it. They can then tell me what I have to do.

EVALUATE YOUR PLAN

Did you follow your plan? *Yes*

Was the outcome as you expected? *Not quite — I needed a letter from the CFS/ME Clinic too — but I got that and I've got an extension!*

Are you satisfied with the result? *Yes, very much.*

Would you use the same solution again? *Yes and next time I'd know what to do.*

PROBLEM-SOLVING SHEET

MY PROBLEM: _____
_____

**ALTERNATIVE
SOLUTIONS
(Think of at least 3)**

**EVALUATE
SOLUTIONS
(What is a possible
result of each
solution?)**

1 _____

1 _____

2 _____

2 _____

3 _____

3 _____

4 _____

4 _____

THE BEST SOLUTION IS NUMBER _____.

MY PLAN TO CARRY OUT THE SOLUTION

_____
_____
_____
_____
_____
_____
_____
_____

EVALUATE YOUR PLAN

Did you follow your plan? _____

Was the outcome as you expected? _____

Are you satisfied with the result? _____

Would you use the same solution again? _____

6

Dealing with other people

Loss of confidence in social situations

When you have CFS/ME, you may become less confident in social situations, such as meeting up with friends or meeting new people, than you were before your diagnosis. This may be because at the moment you are not seeing other people as much as you used to because you are not well. Or you might be worried that your symptoms will make social situations more difficult.

It is understandable that if something makes us feel uncomfortable, we may want to avoid it. However, this can make things worse. If you don't see your friends, it's harder to keep up with what's going on and you may miss opportunities for doing things that you would have enjoyed.

So it is important to try to fight against any lack of confidence and to make an effort to stay in touch with people, even though it may be more difficult than before. People may not know whether they should contact you, so you may need to take the first step and make contact.

If social situations are very tiring for you, it may be best to start with shorter periods of time and build up the length of time as part of your weekly targets.

David

David had become anxious about using the telephone since he became ill. So he began by practising phoning people or places that made him less anxious (e.g. his grandmother). Once he had built up his confidence using the phone, he then felt better about phoning his friends. He realised that he had been nervous about not being able to speak properly but found that people didn't usually notice or mind, even if he did occasionally have difficulty finding the right word.

Jodi

Jodi was worried that she would not have much to say to her friends because she had been indoors resting for so long. But when she did try meeting up with her friends, she found that they didn't expect her to have much news, and they were happy to fill her in on all the gossip from school.

Bullying

Unfortunately anyone can be bullied. If you are already feeling bad because of CFS/ME, bullying can seem even harder to deal with. Bullying may involve people calling you names, hitting, shoving, kicking, sending threatening text messages, making things up to get you into trouble, spreading rumours about you or doing anything else that is intended to upset you.

Bullying by other young people

Bullying is wrong. If you are being bullied, do not blame yourself – it is not your fault. The most important thing is to do something.

- Talk to someone you trust, such as a teacher, parent, older relative or friend. Ask that person not to do anything without telling you first. You have a right to know what is being done for you and to say whether you think it is a good idea.
- Don't give up if the first person you talk to doesn't help. Speak to someone else.
- If you can, write down what has been said or done to you. When you have found someone you can trust, discuss what you have written with that person.

Don't hide what is happening from adults you trust.

Bullying by adults

Adults can bully children in many different ways. If an adult is doing something to you or trying to make you do something that you do not like, then you must talk to someone – even if you are not sure what they are doing is bullying.

If this is happening at school you can talk to your parents. If it is happening at home you could talk to a trusted teacher. Do not keep it a secret.

For further information see the following websites:

Bullying UK: http://www.bullying.co.uk/

Anti-bullying Network: http://www.antibullying.net/

Assertiveness

Being assertive means respecting yourself and others equally.

This contrasts to being passive, which is behaving as if other people's rights matter more than your own, or being aggressive, which is behaving as though your rights matter more than those of others.

We can learn to work towards what we want rather than pushing others around or being a pushover. People will then begin to respond to us differently too.

Asking for something

1 Be clear about what you want
2 Plan and practice
3 Make your request short (e.g. 'That is mine. I want you to give it back.')

Saying 'no'

We have the right to say no.

Work out what you really want to say – listen to your body and feelings.

If you want to say 'no', try to say it early and, if possible, before saying other things. If you are not sure, you can say, 'I don't know. I need more time or more information'.

You don't have to smile or give excuses.

You can offer an alternative, for example, 'No, I don't want to go to the shops with you. Let's go for a walk instead'.

When we say 'no' to someone, we are only refusing their request; we are not rejecting the person.

An assertive body

To have an assertive body, practice keeping eye contact with people and walking tall in front of a mirror. Try it with your family or a friend.

Broken-record method

This can be used when you are asking for something if people are trying to get round you, or when you are not being listened to, or when you want to say 'no'. A broken record sounds like a record stuck in a groove – it goes on and on.

Decide what you want to say and stick to it: 'That is my book and I want it back'. It is possible to be kind first before repeating the statement; for example, 'I am sorry that you do not have a book but that is my book and I want it back'.

A possible broken-record response to being teased is 'I am sorry, I didn't hear you'.

Fogging

Fogging is a way of responding to insults. It is an alternative to simply replying with another insult, which just causes the whole situation to build up.

Fogging swallows up insults like a great fog bank that swallows sights and sounds.

If someone makes hurtful remarks, we don't have to argue or become upset – we can turn ourselves into fog and swallow what they say.

If it's true we can say, 'That's right'.

If it's not true we can answer, 'You could be right' or 'It's possible' or 'You might be right'.

Keep the answers short and bland. It may seem strange at first, but it can be better than becoming very upset or being violent.

If you have been bullied, think about what the bullies say to you and practice 'fogging'.

Relaxation

Being relaxed can help you when you are trying to be more assertive. You can practice relaxing by tensing different muscles and then relaxing them. Lie on the floor; tense and then slowly relax your muscles one by one, starting with your toes and working your way up to your head.

7

Back to school

Dealing with school

Dealing with school can be one of the most important parts of your recovery. If you can get the people at school to be on your side and to help you with your recovery, it can make a big difference. If, on the other hand, they don't know what is going on, you might find that they can be quite unsympathetic, which can make things difficult. This section will help you (1) decide how much school work is right for you at the moment and (2) get the people at school on your side as part of your recovery. We strongly suggest you get your parents to read this section too. They will need to help you communicate what you need to the teachers at your school.

Let's begin with some of the issues that have come up most frequently in our clinic in the last few years.

Frequently asked (school) questions

Q. Some weeks I manage to get to school almost every day for full days, and then other weeks I'm so ill I'm hardly there at all. What should I do? How do I decide what is the right amount of school?

A. Now this sounds like a classic boom-and-bust cycle (see section 'What keeps CFS/ME Going?' in chapter 1): periods when you do a lot followed by spectacular crashes. The way to deal with this is as you would with any boom-and-bust pattern: if you walked 30 minutes on one day and then couldn't walk again for another week, the sensible thing to do would be to walk 5–10 minutes every day. It is the same idea with school. You need to plan a timetable that you think you could stick to most days. There will be a bit of trial and error about this.

For example, we recently saw someone who was very keen to get back into school full-time. Each week she would begin by trying for a full week and would generally make it to Tuesday or Wednesday at the latest before collapsing. This left her feeling very demoralised and depressed. Of course this also relates to having high expectations and using all-or-nothing thinking (see chapter 4, 'Dealing with Unhelpful Thoughts and Attitudes'). She was expecting too much of herself and setting herself up for disappointment.

What she did instead was to start trying five half days. She would get in every morning and come home before lunchtime. She tried this for a week and even *this* was too much. Eventually we settled on three mornings – Monday, Wednesday and Friday. She managed this for three weeks, even though she often felt tired. Over the next few weeks she built up to four half days, then five.

Other people decide to start off with particular subjects rather than specific times before gradually building on them. Either way is good, but you will have to talk about it with your school (see 'Negotiating with the School' later in this chapter).

Q. But if I only go in part-time, won't I fall behind in school work?

A. Yes, you might. But probably no more behind than you are already, if you are already missing quite a lot when you are feeling very unwell. By going in less, but more systematically, and then gradually building on this, you are much more likely to get back to full-time school in the long term. In this way you will definitely catch up eventually. It also means that *you are in control, not the illness*. People recovering from CFS/ME often find it helps to do a little less at first but do it consistently. That way they get back to where they want to be quicker.

The other thing to bear in mind is that catching up is not all about being at school. Including study time in your 'days off' is great practice for getting back to school. The patient described earlier studied for two hours in the morning (with a break) on Tuesdays and Thursdays. In the afternoon she went for a short walk. That way she was getting ready to do more time at school. She was also avoiding the boom-and-bust cycle. Try to structure your off time to have a little activity in it as well as rest times.

Q. I've already fallen so far behind in schoolwork that I'll never catch up.

Q. I've got so many subjects to keep up with that I feel completely overwhelmed.

A. You are not alone! This is probably the most common school problem we have come across. Even people who are perfectly fit and healthy feel overwhelmed by the amount of school work, coursework and exam revision they have to do. The pressure on students at school is often enormous, particularly during exam years. Teachers are also under pressure to get the best results from their pupils. All in all it's not easy for anyone – most people feel stressed and tired at times under that sort of pressure. However, that doesn't mean that you can't do something about it.

You have several options. Firstly you could decide which subjects to prioritise. Look at how to use the Prioritising Chart in chapter 4. In a nutshell, no one can be good at everything. Decide which subjects you need and which subjects you enjoy. Focus on those. You can either drop some of the others or just give them less attention. Another option is to defer some subjects. You might decide, for example, to only do three or four GSCEs this year and catch up with the others later. Remember, in 10 years' time no one is going to care how many GCSEs you have. Do the ones you can. By trying to do too many, you may end up not being able to do any.

You don't need to do it all this year. It might be more sensible to go back a year. This is obviously a big decision with both advantages and disadvantages to it. To start with the disadvantages: a lot of people say they will miss being with their friends, and they are nervous about starting with a whole new bunch of people. Having seen a lot of people through this process, we can say it's never that bad. You tend to see the old friends you like anyway and fit into the new class surprisingly quickly.

The big advantage is it takes the pressure off you. It means you have a whole year, with subjects you know a bit about, to catch up. People often find that the sense of relief outweighs any disadvantages. This in itself can help people feel better. Whatever you choose to do you will need help negotiating with the school.

Q. I'm not going to school at all; is there anything I can do to keep up with work until I get back?

A. Yes, quite a few things. First of all, don't have unrealistic expectations of yourself. It's very difficult to study on your own. Most people need the environment of school to help. *Being in a context where other people are working and learning makes it 10 times easier to work and learn.* Doing it at home alone is tough. Just try and keep up with one or two essentials, not everything.

So get whatever help you can. Your parents may be able to help you get a home tutor (see 'Negotiating with the School' later in this chapter). This can help structure your time and guide your study. Also liaise with the school. Some teachers are very good at suggesting homework and assignments that will help you keep up. Set aside a regular time for study, a time at which you generally feel more alert (often mid- to late morning) and try to stick to it. Again don't expect too much of yourself. The more relaxed you are when you do it, the more you take in. Don't try too hard.

Q. I woke up this morning and could hardly get up, I was so exhausted and in pain. Surely I shouldn't go to school – even if I do, I won't take anything in, so what's the point?

A. First of all, let's put it in context. If you are in the erratic boom-and-bust cycle described earlier (see the first question in this section), then it's a good idea to establish a routine for school before deciding whether you should go.

If you *are* in a routine – and a routine that is, on the whole, reasonable (you are able to stick to it *most* of the time) – then the answer is probably give it a go. Why? Well, people often feel worse than usual first thing in the morning and at the beginning of the week. This is the well-known *Monday Morning Syndrome*. It's a very hard time for anyone to get going, but it is particularly hard if you're already fatigued and exhausted. But not going to school won't necessarily make you feel better and going to school won't necessarily make you feel worse. Believing that you will feel worse if you go to school is a negative prediction, like the ones we talked about in 'What Keeps Us Stuck?' in chapter 4. You are predicting either that it will make you worse or that you won't get anything out of it. That might be true, but it might not. Here's what happened when we explored this idea with one young person (see the text box).

Peter's spirals

Peter was managing to go to school most mornings and come home at lunchtime. However, every so often he would have patches where he couldn't get in at all. He was waking up some days feeling so awful he didn't go to school. When we asked him to explain in more detail he said something like, 'I feel so bad that going will only make me feel worse. I won't be able to concentrate and I'll have to go home anyway'. So he stayed at home and lay on the sofa. This made him feel bored, frustrated, more tired and a bit low. The next day it was harder to go in, and he took that day off too. Soon he was beginning to worry about falling behind and explaining his absence to friends and teachers. This made him feel more low and more ill. He took more time off. After exploring this, we called it his *negative spiral*.

What would happen if he did go in? Well, on days when he had felt bad and had gone in, it hadn't made him feel any better, but it hadn't made him feel much worse either. He then tended to feel better in the next day or two, glad that he hadn't missed school, and he generally felt more on top of things and better about himself. He called this his *positive spiral*. He decided that over all, going to school even when he felt rough was actually less tiring.

What Peter learned was that continuing to go to school even when he felt poorly was less tiring in the long run. This may be the case for you. You might not perform well, you might not take much in, but that doesn't matter. Try not to worry about how much you take in. At first, getting into school is just about getting your body used to a routine again. It's not easy, and of course there will be days when you feel awful, but if you persist it gets easier. If it doesn't, after a few weeks, then you may be trying to do a little too much. Step it down a bit, but don't give up.

Q. How am I going to manage exams? Won't they just kill me?
A. Well they won't be a picnic, but you may be able to manage some of them. First, you can get extra help from the school because of your illness. This allows you extra time and breaks during the exams. This is your right. (See the next section, 'Negotiating with the School'.) Second, decide in

advance how many exams you are going to sit. Be realistic and base it on your current level of ability, not how you would *like* to be. Third, pace yourself. Do a little bit often well in advance of your exam and plan your revision (see 'Study Skills' section). Fourth, remember that everyone gets tired at exam time. They're stressful. Try to plan some fun and some non-study time in the run-up. This may sound silly, but having a cut-off point for studying means that you work in a more focused way. Doing something completely different then gives your 'study brain' a break and means that you come back refreshed rather than already tired. Fifth, expect to be tired. The adrenaline on exam days will get you through, and you'll crash a bit after each one. Try not to be surprised by the 'come down' but remember that the quickest way to recover from a crash is to get back into a routine.

Q. What shall I do on my holidays?

Q. I thought I was better on holiday, but then I got worse when I started back at school. Is that normal?

A. Holidays can be surprisingly tricky. If you watch a runner running a long race, what do they do after they cross the finishing line? Collapse! Holidays can be a bit like that. Coming up to the end of term, people (all of them, even teachers) often begin to flag a bit. The first week of a holiday is often when people get a cold. It's almost like they can let themselves go, can afford to be ill. It's a similar picture on the other side of holidays. The first weeks back at school after a break, particularly the long summer break, are often tough. Again this is true for everyone, not just people with CFS/ ME. Ask your friends – tiredness, headaches, low mood, difficulty getting out of bed – a lot of people (teachers too!) feel pretty rough as they adjust to a new routine.

And routine is the key. The best way to make the transition into and out of holidays easier is to try to keep up a fairly consistent routine throughout that time. So when you are on holiday try to get up at roughly the same time as you do on school days. Now, obviously, if you have to get up at 7:00am for school, that's just not reasonable. But try not to make it too much later. 9:00am at the latest is a good idea. Research seems to show that lying in after 9:00am actually makes people more tired. And try to keep a basic structure – do a bit of physical activity every day, pace the day so that if you are out a lot you have breaks and so on. But most of all have fun. Fun is surprisingly therapeutic.

Negotiating with the school

This is where you need parents or guardians to help. Schools are big institutions, which are often not very good at dealing with individuals in a sensitive way, particularly if that individual has unusual needs or problems. You may have felt that the school has been dismissive of your illness, and you may have felt unsupported by them. Some of the people we have counselled have felt that the school did not really believe they were ill and treated them like 'skivers'. Sad, but all too often true. *Don't take it personally.* As your mum and dad probably know, and you as well, CFS/ME is a hard illness to understand for even medical professionals. From the school's point of view, they see a pupil who turns up every so often looking fine, and then they don't see them again for a few days. They come into some lessons and not others. The trick is to get them to work with you to get you better. The key is communication. Here are some tips and hints on how to get them on your side.

1 Get it in writing

Get the diagnosis of CFS/ME confirmed, in writing, by a professional. First of all, make the diagnosis clear and then say a little bit about what this means. If you are receiving treatment at our unit, we can help you with that. If not, we have included a sample letter. You could take this to your general practitioner and suggest that a letter along these lines would be useful for helping you/ your child return to school. Send this letter to the head teacher, but give copies to the form master/head of year as well. If you feel it necessary, or if there is a particularly unhelpful/suspicious teacher, have copies sent to them too. Let the people that matter know that you/your child is ill. (The sample letter also includes a paragraph on exams that you can delete if unnecessary.)

2 Have a plan

Read over the earlier part of this chapter and take time to decide what the best course of action is – going back a year, dropping some subjects, going in half-time for a while, etc. Discuss it with someone at school. (See the next section, 'Get Someone on Your Side'.) Then get it in writing. Lay out exactly what you are going to try and why. If you want to include it in the letter from your doctor, that's fine. Make sure that all the people who will be involved in this plan know what is going on. Give them a copy of the letter and talk to them if possible.

3 Get someone on your side

There are usually some teachers who are sympathetic and with whom you have a good relationship. A surprising number will know someone with CFS/ME and know a bit about what you are going through. Your school may have someone who specialises in special needs (though remember, that doesn't necessarily mean they will know about CFS/ME). Talk to this person about what you are trying to do and how you are trying to get better. If they seem sympathetic, you might ask if they could help get this across to other members of the staff. It's especially useful to get the head teachers and head of year on your side. That way if anyone else has any problems, you can refer them to the powers that be.

4 Keep them informed

Let them know how things are going for you. If you had planned to get back into school full-time by the end of term and that now seems too difficult, let them know the new plan. You don't have to tell everyone, but talk to the people who matter. If things are going better than you expected, let them know that too.

5 Think about exams

Exams can be a tough time (see the earlier section 'Frequently Asked (School) Questions') and you may need to ask the school for some help. It's normal for people with the kind of situation you have to get extra time and breaks during exams. In extreme cases people can get a room to themselves or even sit them at home. For all of these, you will need a letter from a professional, but we include a sample letter to give them an idea of what might help.

6 Take the pressure off

Particularly if you have been a star pupil, you may have a lot of teachers in different subjects expecting you to do well. It may be worth saying to them explicitly that you are recovering from an illness and that you can't pull out all the stops like you used to. Again, if your parents can communicate this to the teachers, especially if you *are* feeling under pressure to perform, that might ease it a little. (Remember not to pressure yourself either!)

7 Don't expect miracles

Schools are big institutions, as we said, and not often flexible. Don't expect everyone to be on your side or to understand. Expect to have to chase people, repeat yourself and get frustrated. Just patiently keep giving the same message; it will get through. Your main aim is to get the school to agree to a sensible rehabilitation programme for you. Any help you get in addition to that is, as they say, gravy.

Sample Letter

Name
Address
Address
Address
Postcode

To Whom It May Concern:

Re child's name, date of birth, address, address, address, postcode

The above pupil at your school is currently suffering from Chronic Fatigue Syndrome. This is characterised by profound mental and physical exhaustion, muscle and joint pain, poor memory and impaired concentration. Through his/her great personal determination he/she has been able to maintain his/her present level of schoolwork; however, he/she still has significant and disabling trouble with fatigue, pain, impaired concentration and reduced short-term memory.

We are currently working together on a programme of structured rehabilitation for his/her condition. This involves first of all making consistent the amount of activity he/she does from day to day. Once this is achieved we will then gradually, and at his/her pace, build on this. This will involve a graded approach to school return. There is very good evidence that this is the best way to overcome Chronic Fatigue Syndrome, but obviously it will take some time and the cooperation of all parties.

The cognitive impairments and reduced stamina of this condition will affect academic performance, and this should

---

be taken into account in his/her sitting his/her exams. The impact that exam stress has on those with CFS/ME is often profound, but there are several things that can help. Additional help and time with course and homework would be useful. He/she may need longer to sit exams and the opportunity to have a short break during them. If necessary he/she should be allowed to sit exams in a separate area or at home.

Although he/she continues to improve, it will benefit his/her ongoing progress and greatly reduce the likelihood of setback if he/she knows that these measures are agreed and in place.

If you require any further information on this matter please feel free to write or call me.

Schoolwork and exams

Schoolwork and exams can be a major source of worry and stress for people with CFS/ME. Here are some ideas that may help you.

Study skills

Build up gradually

When you have CFS/ME you may feel that your symptoms make studying and revising very difficult. It can be easy to put off these things until you feel ready. But actually the way to become ready is by gradually building up to it. As with other areas that have been discussed in this book, if you have not been doing much studying recently, it is important to start with a small and realistic amount. If you do this small amount every day for a week or two, you may then be ready to increase the length of time. Although it may be difficult at first, remember that concentration and study skills can improve with practice.

Make studying part of your daily routine

Since it can be difficult to motivate yourself to study, it is probably not a good idea to wait until you feel like doing it – instead you may need to make it into a routine. In other words, you choose a particular time of the day when you will be studying.

If you think it would help, you could ask one of your parents to remind you when it is the appropriate time.

Planning – use the salami principle

Whether you've got a big project, a lot of catching up, or revision to do, a good way to plan your work is the salami principle: if you eat the slices one by one you will eventually eat the whole salami. So cut big projects into slices. Set yourself small tasks and you'll eventually complete the large task.

Are you pressuring yourself with very high expectations?

It will be more difficult to study effectively if you are putting yourself under a lot of pressure to do well. Read the section 'High Standards' in chapter 4, and think about whether your expectations are realistic or whether you are putting yourself under too much pressure.

The study period

If you are trying to improve your ability to concentrate and study, there are two main areas to think about: your study environment and the structure of your study sessions.

1 Study environment

Try to make sure that your study environment is conducive to good habits.
- The place where you study is free from distractions.
- The conditions (i.e. chair, desk, temperature and lighting) are suitable for studying.
- The materials you need for studying are all there.

2 Structure for study sessions

- Make each study period not more than about 35 minutes long. This is how long most people can concentrate well. This time may need to be shorter at first if you have not been able to study much recently.
- Develop realistic goals for the study session and write them down.
- Use the 'chocolate box' approach: you may find it easier if you give yourself small chunks to study, with lots of variety, just like a box of chocolates.

- Decide the order in which you will complete tasks.
- At the end of the session spend a few minutes going over again what you have just learned to help you remember it better.
- Plan a simple reward for the end of the study session.

Coping with exams

Long-term planning

Ask yourself, what is it essential to know? Which topics do you know, and where are the gaps in your knowledge?

Write a timetable for your revision, being realistic about how much you can revise in a given time. Plan to revise everything a second time but in a quarter of the time it first took you. Include some extra time for topics that are difficult, or in case you fall behind (this happens to most people).

Remember it's never possible to know *everything*.

Making revision notes

Before you make notes ask yourself how you will use them. Do they need to be detailed so that you don't have to look at the book again or short notes to remind you of the main points? They should suit your needs and include only what you need to know.

Each time you go through the topic, make more condensed notes, so that you have a brief set of notes to revise just before the exam.

Do something with the information you've learned: draw a colourful diagram, explain it to someone else or make recordings of the information. This will help you 'encode' the information more thoroughly in your memory.

Daily strategy

Study one topic at a time for a set amount of time. Stop when the time is up and move on to the next one so that you don't concentrate entirely on one topic and miss out on the others. If you have exam questions from previous years, practice answering them. This will make the exam less daunting.

Make sure you take short breaks throughout the day.

Don't stay up all night revising or drink too much coffee because this may upset your sleep pattern. It's important to eat, sleep and exercise regularly. This will keep you feeling fit and healthy.

Exam day

Look at the notes you've been working from, not at new material, to avoid confusing yourself.

Don't listen to scare-mongering from others, which will stress you unnecessarily. Worrying at this point will not change anything.

When the exam begins, read the instructions and questions carefully and plan your time. If you get stuck in the middle of the exam, start to write notes – this will trigger your memory.

Don't feel you have to write down everything you know and don't feel you have to be a genius – just answer the questions you are asked.

Exam nerves

It's normal to worry before an exam, so don't worry about being very worried! Instead think of yourself as feeling more alert. If you find yourself thinking of all the things that could go wrong, ignore these thoughts – they are a sign of anxiety and you don't have to believe them.

Remember that your exam result will only reflect how you did in that particular exam in that subject. Even if you fail, ask yourself this: Will it matter in 100 years' time? Or even, who will remember in two years' time? This will help you keep the failure in perspective and see it as a temporary setback, not a judgement of you as a person.

Good luck!

8

Severely affected young people with CFS/ME

If you are severely affected by CFS/ME and confined to a wheelchair or a bed, you may feel that it is impossible to get better. It may be difficult to see how even small changes would be possible. However, we have seen many young people improve and even totally recover, including those who had been severely affected. The procedure for change is the same for young people who are severely affected as it is for those who are more active. However, the process will take longer and the goals you set for yourself should be more modest – for instance, set at a lower level of difficulty. There is hope! But change takes time and requires patience and determination.

There are lots of side effects of being confined to a wheelchair or a bed. In addition to the physical side effects such as weakening muscles, constipation and reduced blood flow to your organs, it is likely that you will have lost some of your confidence. However, your body and mind will change and become stronger and livelier again as a result of gradually doing more.

Ideally you will need a therapist or other health professional who can help. Perhaps talk to your parents about requesting a referral to a specialist service if they have not already done so. If there isn't one available, the local physiotherapy team may be able to help.

Activity levels

Whether you are in bed all day or part of the day, the aim is to do a little bit of activity regularly – about four times a day. For example you may start by sitting up in bed every three hours for about 10 minutes. If you are able to sit up, the first step may be to get out of bed and sit in a chair twice a day for 30 minutes. Try walking to the toilet if you are bed-bound. If your muscles are hurting, some light stretching and strengthening exercises may help. Again it is important that you do the exercises every day. Doing a little bit often is better than doing a lot once a week. You may find talking difficult. If so, try to talk for short periods of time to start with before building up to longer times. Choose new topics to talk about. Try not to focus your discussion on how you are feeling. Although it is understandable that you have been discussing how you feel with your family, it often makes people feel worse in the long term.

Even if you are not leaving the house, it is helpful to do what you would do if you were planning to leave the house (e.g. get dressed during the day to separate the day from night). Have a winding-down period at night before you sleep. Have a shower in the morning to wake you up and a bath at night to relax. Try to eat three meals a day even if they are small portions. The routine is important.

The goals you choose may feel difficult at first but you should feel that they are achievable. You should avoid 'booming and busting' – i.e. doing a lot one day and crashing the next. You will undoubtedly feel worse before you feel better, and it is likely that your muscles will feel sore and tired when you start to use them. Your fatigue may also seem worse but the symptoms will reduce if you stick to a routine.

Once you are able to consistently achieve the goals you have set for yourself (e.g. 80 per cent of the time), you should increase your activity a little, by no more than 10 per cent. Remember: it doesn't matter how little you do at the start – it's the consistency that's important. If you have a bad day, try to put it behind you and start afresh the next day with a new attitude. Every day is a new day. Progress is bound to be imperfect. Don't give up.

As you improve, the thought of going back to school or college will feel daunting and maybe even impossible. However, when you start the process of change, don't focus on the end goal – think of what you are doing now. The good thing about being young is that you are more adaptable than older people. No matter how bad you may feel now, it is possible to change. You may want to consider a range of options: if you are 16, this may include college, voluntary work or part-time work. The important thing is that you do what feels right for you.

Sleep

It is highly likely that your sleep routine will be disturbed. People who sleep well usually have a good sleep routine as well as good routines of activity during the day. Again, although it's difficult, try not to sleep during the day because every bit of sleep you get during the day will affect your sleep at night. Resting is different from sleeping. You need to intersperse activity with rest but not sleep.

It will help if you choose your own structure for yourself. Try not to let your body dictate what you do. We suggest that you put yourself in charge of your own rehabilitation. Remember that it doesn't matter how long it takes, but it is important to keep active and very gradually increase the amount you are doing.

9

The future

Making further gains

Building on improvements

We hope that by using this book you will have learnt some skills to help you work on problems by yourself.
Here are some reminders:

- Take things gradually.
- Set yourself weekly targets, broken down into manageable chunks.
- Once you can do your target activity without feeling too tired, keep it as part of your normal routine.

Watch out for unhelpful thoughts

For example, you might find yourself thinking that you can't do it. Feeling afraid is normal but it does not mean you are going to fail. Keep diaries of these unhelpful thoughts, as well as the more helpful ones.

Remember that you've made a lot of progress if you've come this far. There is no reason why you shouldn't be able to take the final steps to recovery.

Setbacks are normal

It's not unusual to have a setback, which is when you have an increase in symptoms for several days and can't keep up with the things you normally do.
When this happens, it is easy to panic about what this means. You may worry that your condition has taken a turn for

the worse or that you are not getting better at all. You may start to feel down about this.

However, it is important to remember the following:

Feeling worse generally does *not* mean that your condition has gotten worse.

You can't always avoid having a setback, but these can be dealt with quite easily.

The important thing is to be able to recognise a setback if it occurs and to tackle it by taking some positive action.

Things that can trigger setbacks

Setbacks can happen for no particular reason, but often they occur after something else has happened, such as

- an infection or another illness;
- stressful events, e.g. exams, changing schools, a major argument with your best friend, being rejected by someone you like;
- working towards deadlines, e.g. for handing in coursework;
- family difficulties;
- your mood has become low or depressed;
- you have stopped using the strategies you have learnt in treatment and have gone back to your old ways of doing things.

These kinds of things can increase fatigue. They may also reduce the chance that you will carry out your regular planned activities and relaxation.

Although having a setback may seem like a disaster at the time, it can help you to understand your CFS/ME better and improve the way that you deal with it in the future. Most people overcome their setbacks quite easily and go on to make further progress. The important thing is not to panic!

How to tackle setbacks

During an infection

If you have an infection your CFS/ME symptoms may get worse. You should expect this. If you have taken your temperature and find it to be high, then you should rest for a while. If you are feeling weak but don't have a temperature, you should cut out your sporting activities. If you have a cold you should try to carry on as usual.

Focus on what is most important

If you do not have time to carry out your programme or do not feel able to do so, do not give up. Instead, think about what the most important parts of your programme are and focus on those, adapting them if necessary, until you can get back on track again. It may be helpful to talk to your parents about how to adjust your programme at times like these.

Keep balanced

Remember to balance your days as much as possible in terms of activities and relaxation.

Be kind to yourself

Are you asking too much of yourself at this time? You may need to lower your expectations. Remember to praise yourself for any achievements, no matter how small.

Exam time

Exams can be a difficult time for people with CFS/ME. That's why we've included a separate section on coping with exams. Read this at least six weeks before your exams start.

Difficulties with friends

Disagreements or arguments with friends can be upsetting. Everybody has problems like these from time to time. They are normal and help you learn about relationships. If you find yourself worrying a lot, write down your worries. Then write down a different way of looking at the situation. It can be helpful to talk to your mum or dad, another family member or a friend about them.

Preventing setbacks

There will be times when it is more difficult to cope with your fatigue. To try to prevent a setback, it may be helpful for you to complete the following:

What are the kinds of things that make my fatigue worse?

What are the warning signs that my CFS/ME is getting worse?

If I get into difficulties, what steps should I take?

What have you learnt about your CFS/ME symptoms?

You may find it helpful to complete this page as you get towards the end of the programme, in order to help sum up what you have learnt.

1 **What things may have contributed to your developing this condition in the first place?** (e.g. virus or infections, being worried about problems, having very high standards, etc.)

2 **What factors may have been acting to keep your CFS/ME symptoms continuing or slowing down your recovery?** (e.g. staying in bed all the time, pushing yourself too hard on good days, expecting too much from yourself)

3 **What things have you found to be helpful from working through this book?** (e.g. having a set wake-up time, having regular breaks, being easier on yourself, gradually building up your exercise)

4 **What areas do you still need to work on?** (e.g. targets for treatment you have not yet achieved, such as going back to school full-time; resting at regular times; learning to worry less)

Targets for the next three months

Please write down targets that you plan to work towards during the next three months.

What do you need to do to make sure you will be able to reach these targets?
(e.g. work out a programme for gradually building up the amount of time spent at school, seeing friends or doing exercise, etc.).

Three-month follow-up

It may be helpful to fill in this page at the end of the three-month follow-up period.

1 How far have you gotten with the three-month targets you listed on the previous page? Please go through each in turn:

2 Did you have any difficulties? If so, what were they?

3 What areas do you still need to work on?

Targets for six months

Targets to work towards during the next three months (i.e. between your three-month and six-month reviews):

Things you need to do to make sure you will be able to reach these targets:

Six-month review

1 How far have you gotten with the three-month targets you listed on the previous page? Please go through each in turn:

2 Did you have any difficulties? If so, what were they?

3 What areas do you still need to work on?

Further targets

After your six-month review point you are likely to have further targets to work towards – you may like to write them here.

Targets:

Things you need to do to make sure you will be able to reach these targets:

Learning from the experience of CFS/ME

Often people say that the experience of having CFS/ME, although very difficult, has taught them useful things. There are some examples in the following box.

Samina

Samina was always on the go before she developed CFS/ME. Once she was better, she still liked to have a lot going on, but she was careful to take more time to chill out and relax.

Jon

Jon had been a perfectionist, always wanting to do things to a high standard. As he managed his CFS/ME, he learnt that although having high standards is okay, it's not helpful to pursue them so much that you become exhausted or ill. He learnt to be more flexible and let go of perfectionist standards when he could see they would make him stressed, unhappy or fatigued.

Sarah

Sarah had always been a bit of a worrier, going over and over things in her mind. When she developed CFS/ME, she began to talk to her friends and family more about her worries and found that this was usually more helpful than trying to deal with her worries on her own.

What have you learnt as a result of your experiences with CFS/ME?

It may be useful to think about this so that you can apply the lessons to your future. If you like, write some of the things you've learnt here.

Keeping up improvements

To keep up the improvements you have made, such as the activities you practise, *make them part of your everyday life.*

- Make sure your days are balanced between activity and rest.
- Don't fall back into the trap of the boom-and-bust cycle by doing too much some days and too little on others.
- Keep up your regular sleep routine.
- Continue with at least 30 minutes of exercise two to three times a week. This will keep you fit.
- Keep your expectations of yourself at a reasonable and realistic level.
- Praise yourself for what you achieve rather than always focusing on what there is still to be done.

Final note

Making the changes discussed in this book is not easy. They take a lot of hard work, time and courage.

There will be times when it doesn't go well, but it's the overall picture you need to focus on. If you have a setback for any reason, don't be too hard on yourself. No one can do things perfectly all the time.

Good luck!

10

Information for parents and other caregivers

Having a child with CFS/ME may at times be worrying, frustrating and stressful. It is often difficult for parents to know the best thing to do, especially in the face of lack of understanding, conflicting advice or even disbelief from others.

We hope that reading the self-help guide will show you how to proceed with helping your child to recover, and help to reduce any confusion. Here are some additional points that you may wish to consider in conjunction with earlier sections of this book (also see the section 'Negotiating with the School' in chapter 7). Your support and guidance can make an enormous difference in helping the young person get better, particularly in helping them to achieve the right balance between activity and rest and to gradually build up their activities.

Praise and encouragement

Give lots of encouragement when the child makes efforts to carry out targets from their programme. The treatment can be difficult at times, so the more support the better.

Give praise for any achievement the child makes, no matter how small. This will help the child realise that they are making progress even if they are still nowhere near back to normal. Achievements such as walking for five minutes or getting up half an hour earlier may not seem like much, but they are signs of improvement.

Remember that the treatment is likely to cause the symptoms to become worse in the short term, until the child's body has begun to build up more strength and tolerance. The increase in symptoms can be distressing, both for the child and for parents. One of the ways in which parents can be helpful is to encourage them to continue with their activity programme despite their symptoms. In the past it may have been the case that the child's behaviour has become dependent on how bad the symptoms are. Your child may now need help carrying out their programme regularly, not just on good days. When giving praise, it is best to be very clear and specific about the behaviour that you are praising.

How much you should encourage

Some parents report that they don't know how much they should be reminding or encouraging their child to carry out their goals. If this is the case, it may be helpful to discuss the issue with your child, and ask how you can best help them carry out their goals. They may feel that they want encouragement on some things (e.g. helping them get up on time) but not on others (e.g. exercise). It is possible that they will need more encouragement particularly at the beginning of the programme.

Your child is not doing what they agreed

If your child is repeatedly not managing to do what they have agreed you could check the following:

1 Does the current goal relate to one of your child's longer-term goals?
2 Was the goal too ambitious? If so, think about how it would be possible to reduce the behaviour so that it is manageable at this stage.
3 Is there something blocking your child from being able to achieve the goal, such as fear of making the symptoms worse or fear of what other people may think?

Your child wants to do *more* than has been agreed

Sometimes your child may want to do too much. This usually happens on a good day when they are feeling better. It is important to encourage them to stick to their programme. Otherwise, doing too much can lead to an unacceptable level of increased symptoms, delay progress and cause a setback.

You think you may be doing too much for your child

When you are trying to support a child with CFS/ME, it can be difficult to know how much you should help and how much you should leave the child to do things for themselves. Often parents are concerned that the child's symptoms will worsen if the child pushes themselves too far, which can result in the parents sometimes doing too much for the child. Or the parent may be more involved in the child's day-to-day life than would usually be the case for a young person of that age. This is entirely understandable. If you think this is your situation, you can plan how to gradually reduce the number of things that you are doing for your child and how to help them manage more on their own. Becoming more independent and seeing more of people outside of the family is an important part of the recovery process.

Dealing with your own worries about your child's symptoms

It is natural to be concerned about your child's symptoms. Sometimes, however hard you try, your own worries might leak out and can be picked up by others, including your children. If so, you may want to work on containing your own worries and focus on helping the child recover. This might involve practising accepting the things that you cannot personally change and tolerating uncertainty. You could ask your partner to support you by pointing out, in a kind rather than a critical way, if your own worries may be becoming visible to the child.

Parents can have worrying thoughts, such as 'What if my child never gets better?' or 'What if I cause a relapse by encouraging my child to do things that she doesn't want to do?' or 'She is looking more tired; maybe she will have a setback if she's not careful'. You cannot stop such thoughts popping into your mind, but with practice, it can be possible to simply notice them as thoughts that may not necessarily be factually correct. Or it might be helpful to think about reasons why they are not true, for example, remembering times when your child has experienced worsening fatigue without having a full setback. Reminding yourself that temporary increases in fatigue is a normal part of the recovery process may also help.

Sometimes parents find it helpful to write down a list of their worries about their child and come up with alternative ways of dealing with the situation in a problem-solving way. This involves focusing on solutions or ways of coping if the feared outcome did occur.

Your child has very high standards

One of the factors that may put children and young people at risk for developing CFS/ME is the tendency to set very high standards for themselves. Often these individuals push themselves harder than others do and put more pressure on themselves. Obviously this may have advantages: they achieve good grades at school, or do well at sports or hobbies or become someone who often helps other people. However, sometimes the pressure can be counterproductive and cause the child to become stressed and fatigued, thus achieving less than he or she would otherwise manage.

As parents, it is natural to be very proud of their achievements. However, for parents of a child with CFS/ME, who may be particularly sensitive to issues of success and failure, it is helpful to address such issues. Sometimes children are so keen to make their parents proud that they become fearful of letting their parents down or disappointing them. Other children are particularly focused on what people outside of the family (e.g. their peers, teachers or future employers) will think of them if they do not do well. Either way, such issues are worth discussing.

As adults we may think it goes without saying that we will love, respect and accept our children no matter what they achieve or don't achieve. However, some children do not always completely believe this. Or they may believe that they will not be able to have a happy and successful life if they do not get the school grades they would like. Some children will therefore need extra support in helping them realise that they will be good, acceptable and loveable people regardless of how much they achieve in terms of academic grades or in other areas. For some children, one discussion may be sufficient. Others will need ongoing reminders and support.

Use of reward systems

It may be helpful to remember the principles of reinforcement. If the consequences of a particular behaviour are rewarding or favourable to a child, that behaviour is likely to continue or increase in strength (e.g. become more frequent). It is therefore important to give your child lots of praise for meeting the targets set in their activity programme or for doing their best to meet the targets.

Sometimes this process of reinforcement can happen in relation to the amount of attention that you give your child. Most children crave attention from their parents, of any type. Sometimes parents can find themselves giving children more attention when they are badly behaved, which may have the unwanted effect of increasing the undesired behaviour. For example, one young person was in a very busy family and would get attention only when his behaviour became quite extreme (e.g. throwing and breaking things).

Sometimes we can reinforce certain behaviours in our children without meaning to. For example, if a child has difficulties sleeping and his mother keeps him company when he wakes up during the night, this may increase the chances of the child waking up and wanting attention, because the mother's company was enjoyable for the child. So even though the mother is trying to help the child by comforting them or providing company when they wake in the night, she is providing positive reinforcement for 'waking' behaviour. Therefore, if you want the child to sleep during the night, it is important not to inadvertently 'reward' them if they wake up.

It may be helpful to consider whether there are any ways in which you may be unwittingly reinforcing some unwanted behaviours in your child despite trying to be helpful. If you do think that this is the case, you may need to set yourself targets to reduce such behaviours (gradually if appropriate).

This process can happen with symptoms too. Sometimes children learn that when they report symptoms they get more attention and care. However, talking about symptoms a lot can actually make the child feel worse and more focused on their symptoms in the long run. If this might be the case, it is important that the child gets plenty of attention and care in situations *not* related to their symptoms.

When a child has a chronic condition it can be easy for conversations to revolve around the illness. It is helpful to make sure that there are conversations every day with your child that have nothing to do with how they are feeling, such as about a TV programme they are watching or an interest they have.

It may be possible to use the principles of positive reinforcement to encourage new, more helpful behaviours. Reinforcement does not have to be anything large. It can include things such as smiles, hugs, praise or positive attention. Although it is better to use 'natural' reinforcement from the environment, in the early stages it may be helpful to set up an 'artificial' reinforcement system if your child is finding particular behaviours very difficult. An example of a natural reinforcement would be having a good time with a friend if the child managed to walk for 10 minutes to get to the friend's house, whereas an artificial reinforcement would be if the child was given some money if they managed to walk for 10 minutes. Thus, for a child who does not like exercise, knowing that they will get a small reward (e.g. to rent a video of their choice or have their favourite meal) at the end of the week if they achieve their exercise targets may help encourage them. (Remember that using sweets or chocolate as a reward could result in unhealthy eating habits or weight gain!) Over time, they may learn that they feel better and can do more things when they are fitter, so the 'natural' reinforcement will take over and the 'artificial' reinforcements can be phased out.

Try to make sure that you are on the lookout for examples of good behaviour that can be reinforced in everyday life. For example, one parent noticed that his son was talking nicely with his sister in the car rather than teasing her. He was immediately rewarded by having the choice of radio programme that the family listened to for the next 20 minutes. Positive reinforcement of good behaviour can result in very quick results! It is important for the reward to happen immediately after the good behaviour.

When you want to help a child to change their behaviour, focus on no more than two or three examples at a time. This helps both you and your child stay focused on the good behaviours that need reinforcing. At the start, you need to reinforce good behaviour very frequently for long-term change to occur. Lots of praise and rewarding can feel unnatural or abnormal but it is important. Remind yourself that it will not have to continue at such a high frequency forever.

Setting boundaries

It is not unusual to find it difficult to set firm boundaries, even if your child is well. It can be even harder when you can see that your child is unwell or unhappy. For example, if your child wakes up in the morning and they report feeling too unwell to go to school, this can put the parent in a difficult situation. Some parents report that when they try to encourage the child to get up, the child starts complaining more about their symptoms, or resisting or becoming angry or distressed. This can be distressing for the parent, and it can feel easier to back down and let the child stay at home. The young person is then not learning how to manage to get up and go to school even though they are feeling tired, unwell, anxious or unmotivated. Often young people will feel at their worst when they have just woken up, so it is important not to change one's plans or predict how the rest of the day is going to be based on those feelings. The child has also learnt that they or their symptoms are in charge rather than their parent. Therefore, it is important that this cycle is reversed.

If there are two parents, it is helpful for both parents to present a united front. The night before, all concerned should agree about the time the child needs to get up the next morning. It should be made clear that this will take place regardless of how the child is feeling in the morning. It can be helpful to discuss how the young person would feel best supported in getting up in the morning; for instance, would they prefer to be woken up by parents or an alarm clock, would they appreciate a parent checking in a few minutes later to see that they have managed to get up or would they prefer to be left alone to get up on their own. Which family member would the young person prefer to help them? The key thing is that there is agreement about what time the young person will get up and that this will take place regardless of how they are feeling. Any other specific details are negotiated with the young person.

It can be difficult for parents to see their child going to school when they are feeling fatigued or stressed, but in the long term it is important for the child to learn how to attend school even if they are not fully well. Some adults have reported that if their parents often let them miss school when they had symptoms, this continued into their adult life. They often took days off work because it had become a habit or a learnt way of coping with symptoms or stress.

Similar principles apply to other situations where the young person is trying to avoid something they need to do. For example, they may want to get out of doing exercise or household chores and may become argumentative or anxious. It is important to agree on house rules in advance and be clear about what is not acceptable. An example of this may be the amount of time spent on the computer or tablet. When rules are broken, penalties must be carried out. These penalties should be specified in advance and carried out, rather than being empty threats. When you make a rule, you have to mean it and stick to it!

Your child lacks confidence in social situations

Some young people with CFS/ME have always been shy. Other children may become less confident in social situations if they miss out on school or socialising because of their symptoms. It can be helpful to find a moment to talk to your child about the issues they are having regarding socialising. Try to identify exactly what the problem is: Are they worried about how to keep a conversation going, or about standing up for themselves or saying 'no' or about expressing their feelings or needs?

Helping your child problem-solve about how to make such situations easier can be very useful. You could encourage them to try out small changes in behaviour, in less difficult situations to start with. For example, they might want to practise how to look interested in another person, how to ask another person questions and listen carefully to the reply, how to find things they have in common with another person and how to leave conversations politely.

Effects of CFS/ME on parents

Having a child with CFS/ME can be a very stressful experience for parents. It can be helpful to discuss your feelings with a trusted friend, relative, teacher or GP. You may want to read chapter 4, "Dealing with Unhelpful Thoughts and Attitudes', because parents have these thoughts too! It is easy to feel pessimistic or down about the situation. If this is the case, practise identifying and challenging your negative thoughts in the way described. It is important to remember that children can and do recover from CFS/ME, even if it seems like a slow process.

Remember to take time for yourself each day, doing something pleasurable that is just for you. This will help you feel better and may also help to show to your child that everyone needs time to relax and enjoy themselves.

Stress in parents

When your child is unwell, it is very easy to focus all of your attention on their needs, thereby inadvertently neglecting your own needs. Children learn by observation and without being aware of that learning. Therefore, by taking good care of yourself, you will be setting a great example for your children. This means eating healthily, taking some regular exercise and seeing friends.

There may be lots of other stress in your life, such as work stress, relationship difficulties or caring for elderly parents or other family members. This may have an impact on the smooth running of the household and the atmosphere at home. Stress cannot be avoided entirely, but if you are feeling overwhelmed or having difficulty coping this can result in depression or high levels of anxiety. In this situation it is important that you get help for yourself. If talking to your friends is not enough on its own or does not feel right for you, the next step may be to talk to your GP. Your doctor will be able to advise about different options such as counselling or other types of support or perhaps antidepressants. There is evidence that both talking therapies and antidepressants are effective treatments for depression. Cognitive behaviour therapy is the treatment of choice for anxiety disorders. There are also self-help books available through Books on Prescription at your local library, such as the Overcoming series by Constable and Robinson.

Illness in parents or family members

If parents or other family members have a physical illness, sometimes the child can assume that all physical symptoms are potentially worrying and a sign of a serious disease. For example, one child became worried about her own symptoms and health after seeing her grandmother becoming ill with heart disease. Children may not necessarily talk about these fears so parents may not be aware of them.

It is important to emphasise to the child that most symptoms are very common and are usually not a sign of anything serious. Often they happen without any obvious cause, or sometimes stress can cause physical symptoms. This can include the child feeling pressured at school or simply having high standards for themselves.

Giving up things in your own life to help a child with CFS/ME

It is not unusual for parents, especially mothers, to give up things in their own life in order to care for their child with CFS/ME. This might be work or leisure activities. As your child begins to get better and can become more independent, parents may need to increase the amount of things they do for themselves and begin to return to previous activities. This can be very helpful for both the child and the parent.

Parents of severely affected young people with CFS/ME

If your child is severely affected, you may worry they will never get better. This is natural. However, it is possible for your child to get better, which you can help them to do. You do need help though from a health professional who understands CFS/ME.

One of the difficulties associated with CFS/ME is the loss of strength that results from long-term rest. In addition, if your child is lying down in bed for a prolonged period, they will probably feel dizzy, weak and fatigued when they get up. However, the problem can be overcome by gradually and consistently building up activities. As your child starts to do more, symptoms will wax and wane. If they experience a worsening of symptoms you may be worried that their illness is being made worse by the activity. However, we expect this to happen at times and it is important to keep focused and get back on track even if there has been a temporary setback.

Although you yourself may feel extremely concerned, it is important that you try to keep focused on the programme and the set routines. Your child will take their confidence from you. If you are committed they are more likely to be also. It is important to reward their progress, no matter how small, as you go along and encourage them when it gets difficult. At the same time you have to remember that you are the parent and at times you will have to set boundaries. When you make a rule, you have to mean it and stick to it. This may include being clear about how long they spend on a computer, how to talk to other members of the family or what time they go to bed.

With regard to gradually increasing activity, consistency is key. Start realistically. At first your child may only be able to sit up out of bed for 10 minutes twice a day. It is important, though, that they eat in the dining room or kitchen, not in their bedroom, as soon as possible.

Although it may seem impossible when you start, the same principles that have been described in the rest of this book can be applied to children and young people who are severely affected. The important thing is that the goals and routines are realistic and manageable for your child's current level of strength and abilities, and that they are built up gradually.

Psychological problems

Being a teenager can bring many challenges, including exams, changes in relationships with their peers, a changing physical appearance, having a boyfriend or girlfriend, becoming more independent from their parents, developing their own beliefs and values, beginning to work, making decisions about the future and so on.

Given all these changes and challenges, it is normal for teenagers to experience mood swings, to feel confusion about themselves and others, to argue with their friends and parents, to experiment with different ways of doing things and more.

Sometimes parents find it difficult to work out whether their child is going through normal difficulties, or whether they are developing problems for which professional help may be needed (e.g. depression, anxiety, eating disorders).

If your child's difficulties are causing significant distress or are interfering with their ability to carry out schoolwork, relationships, household chores, hobbies and other activities, then it would be advisable to address the issue.

Depression

Depression is defined as the presence of five or more of the following symptoms nearly every day for at least two weeks:

* low mood or irritability lasting most of the day,
* lack of interest or pleasure in previously enjoyed activities most of the day,
* appetite change,
* lack of energy,
* sleep disturbance,
* feelings of worthlessness or excessive guilt,
* agitated activity or appearing 'slowed down',
* recurrent thoughts of death and
* difficulties concentrating or making decisions.

Since children and young people may not be able to express or understand many of the symptoms that would indicate depression in adults, parents should be aware of some other behaviours that could signal depression in a child: a sudden drop in school performance, outbursts of shouting or crying, aggression, antisocial behaviour and the use of alcohol or other drugs. Obviously some of the symptoms of depression (e.g. sleep disturbance, lack of energy, concentration problems) overlap with those of CFS/ ME, which makes diagnosis more complicated. Treatment is essential for children and young people struggling with depression so they can be free to develop the necessary academic and social skills.

Anxiety

Issues with anxiety may focus on a particular situation or theme, such as social situations, going outdoors, being separated from a parent or loved one, blood or injections, spiders or snakes. Or the anxiety may be more generalised, with the child worrying about lots of different topics. If the anxiety occurs after a traumatic event, the child may experience nightmares or intrusive memories of the event. Sometimes children become obsessional about washing or checking things or they show other repeated behaviours. Anxiety may be regarded as problematic if the child finds it very distressing or it interferes with their normal routine, school life, social activities or relationships. Alternatively, if they are avoiding certain situations because of their anxiety, this avoidance itself may be causing interference with normal activities.

Eating disorders

With regard to eating disorders, the following can be warning signs: significant weight loss or failure to make expected weight gain during a period of growth; intense fear of gaining weight or becoming fat; self-esteem unduly influenced by body weight or shape; in females, the absence of three consecutive menstrual periods; excessive amounts of time exercising; lying about having eaten food; bingeing; sense of lack of control of eating during bingeing; deliberate vomiting and laxative use.

Self-harm

Any attempts by children to harm themselves (e.g. cutting), even if they do not intend to kill themselves, should be taken very seriously. Further professional help should be sought through your GP. Please do the same if your child expresses suicidal thoughts; if they seem to be at immediate risk you can take them to A&E.

If you are worried that your child may be suffering from one of these problems, or another psychological difficulty, please see your child's GP.

Summary for parents

- Your child will need help in maintaining *consistent* levels of activity, carrying out the same routine on both good and bad days. Encourage them to carry out the usual activities even on bad days and *not* to do more on good days.

- The programme is likely to result in an increase in symptoms in the short term. Your child will need your support in continuing with their activity programme despite the increased symptoms.
- Give lots of praise when they work towards their targets.
- Remind them that their worth as a human being does not depend upon school or other achievements.
- Take breaks and look after yourself too.

11

Other problems

When you need to seek help

Just like other people, individuals with CFS/ME can sometimes experience difficulties such as relationship problems, anxiety, depression and eating disorders. Whether it is you or a friend or relative who is having problems, these problems are real, and they deserve to be treated. They are not a sign of weakness. They are not something you can 'just snap out of' even if you try.

When you find yourself in these types of situations, it is a good idea to talk to someone whom you can trust, such as a parent, relative, friend, teacher or your GP. It can make a big difference to have someone who understands what you are going through, and often they will be able to think of ways to help you overcome your difficulties.

You may be concerned that your problems are not serious enough to talk about with someone else. But if they are causing you distress or are interfering with your normal daily life, it is worth seeking further help.

Research has shown that males can find it harder to look for and accept help than females. Whether you are male or female, it's okay to ask for help and receive it.

A list of resources at the end of this book includes telephone numbers and websites of organisations that might be able to help you.

You don't have to suffer alone. There will always be someone willing to listen and help.

Further resources

CFS/ME information

Self-help books for adults:

> *Coping with Chronic Fatigue* by Trudie Chalder (Sheldon Press, 1995)
> *Overcoming Chronic Fatigue* by Mary Burgess and Trudie Chalder (Robinson, 2005)

General resources for young people

We do not endorse any of these organisations or websites – they are included for information only. Please check carefully before taking any advice from them. The following information was correct at the time that this book went to press, but you may need to search online if information becomes out of date.

ChildLine

Children and young people may phone and write to ChildLine about anything – no problem is too big or too small. Some of the things children phone about are feeling lonely or unloved, worries about their future, problems about school, bullying, drugs, pregnancy, HIV and AIDS, physical and sexual abuse, running away and concerns about parents, brothers, sisters and friends. When you phone ChildLine you will be able to talk to a counsellor – someone who will listen to you and help you find ways to sort out your problems and worries in confidence. If you want, the counsellor can put you in touch with other people who can also help you.

Because ChildLine is an 0800 number, calls are free and don't show up on a BT or cable phone bill. Calls also don't show up on the bill for some mobile phone networks: check on the ChildLine website for up-to-date information about the different networks. If you are worried about this, try to call from a phone box.

Telephone helpline: ChildLine (free, 24 hours a day): 0800 1111. Website: http://www.childline.org.uk. On this website you can chat with a ChildLine counsellor online through an instant messaging format called '1–2–1 chat', or you can post on a message board to get support and advice from other young people.

Supportline

Supportline offers confidential emotional support to children and young adults about a vast range of topics such as mental health, drugs, child abuse, bullying, sexuality, bereavement, self-harm and many other issues.

You can get in touch with Supportline via their helpline – 01708 765200 – or you can email info@supportline.org.uk.

They also provide links to other support services which can help you with any problems you are facing. Visit the website at http://www.supportline.org.uk/.

Youth Access

To find out about information, advice, counselling and support services specifically for young people in your area, you can call Youth Access on 020 8772 9900 or look on their website: http://www.youthaccess.org.uk/.

Help with specific difficulties

Bullying

Bullying Online provides advice about how to deal with bullying at home, at school and over the Internet: http://www.bullying.

co.uk/. Call the helpline for advice on 0808 800 2222. For tips on how to prevent or deal with bullying go to http://www.antibullying. net/.

Bereavement

If you or someone you know has suffered the loss of a loved one, you can contact the Child Bereavement Trust for support and advice: 01494 568900 (telephone) or http://www.child-bereavement.org.uk.

Winston's Wish is a charity for young people who have lost a loved one. Their website provides support and answers to common questions surrounding loss, and you can also ask your own questions to be answered online. Visit the website: http://foryoungpeople.winstonswish.org.uk/.

Mental health

Young Minds is a children's mental health charity. Their website, www.youngminds.org.uk, has a lot of help and advice about how to deal with depression, anxiety and different kinds of feelings and emotions, as well information about the services available for young people with mental health issues.

Samaritans: For people who feel suicidal, troubled or in despair. Available 24 hours a day. Call on 08457 90 90 90; email jo@samaritans.org; or write to Freepost RSRB-KKBY-CYJK, Chris, PO Box 90 90, Stirling, FK8 2SA. http://www.samaritans. org/.

Sex

Sexwise is a free and confidential helpline on sex, relationships and contraception for young people in the United Kingdom. Tel. 0800 282930, 7:00am to 12:00 midnight daily

Brook Advisory Centres is a confidential service for people under 25 that provides information regarding pregnancy testing, contraception, missed periods, termination and sexually transmitted diseases. You can search for your nearest service online: http://www.brook.org.uk.

THT Direct–Specialist HIV Service (Tel. 0808 802 1221) is a specialist HIV telephone information and advice service provided by Terrence Higgins Trust (THT). For more information, see http://www.tht.org.uk.

Sexuality

The Lesbian and Gay Foundation provides a wide range of advice and support about many issues for lesbian, gay and bisexual people. See http://www.lgf.org.uk/.

Eating disorders

Beat: Beat provides helplines, online support and a network of UK-wide self-help groups to help adults and young people in the United Kingdom beat their eating disorders.

Website: http://www.b-eat.co.uk

Adult helpline: 0845 634 1414, open Monday through Friday

Youthline: 0845 634 7650, open Monday through Friday

You can also text the Youthline Service on 07786 201820 and they will call you back within 24 hours.

Drugs

Frank (www.talktofrank) offers information and advice to anyone in the United Kingdom concerned about drugs. They have a daily 24-hour contact service which is free and confidential.

Alcohol

Alateen (http://www.al-anonuk.org.uk/public/what-alateen) provides a confidential helpline for young people aged 12–20 who have been affected by someone else's drinking.

Alcohol Concern has lots of information and advice on drinking and alcohol-related problems on its website: http://www.alcoholconcern.org.uk.

You can also call the free national drink helpline (Drinkline) if you are concerned about your own drinking or that of a family member or a friend. Tel. 0300 123 1110.

National Association for Children of Alcoholics (NACOA) has a free helpline for children of alcoholics which provides listening, advice and links with other services. It also offers help to children who are concerned about their parent's use of drugs and provides advice and information to professionals. Tel. 0800 358 3456, http://www.nacoa.org.uk.

Resources for parents and caregivers

We do not endorse any of these organisations or websites. They are included for information only, and readers are advised to check carefully before taking any advice from them.

Family Lives

A national charity offering help and information for all aspects of family life. They provide a 24-hour helpline, advice website, email service, live chat service and parenting support groups.
Website: http://www.familylives.org.uk
Telephone helpline: 0808 800 2222
An email support service is available at the website.

Advisory Centre for Education (ACE)

ACE is an independent national advice centre for parents of children in state schools.
Website: http://www.ace-ed.org.uk

Children's Legal Centre

Free legal advice line for children and adults on any aspect of law affecting a child. Includes advice and representation for children and adults involved in education disputes or Local Education Authority.
Website: http://www.childrenslegalcentre.com

Citizens Advice

Local offices can offer practical advice on benefits, debt management, housing, and so on.
Website: http://www.citizensadvice.org.uk

Young Minds

Free, confidential service for parents and carers who are worried about the emotional well-being of their child.
Website: http://www.youngminds.org.uk
Parent helpline: 0808 802 5544

Bullying

If your child is being bullied, the following websites provide information and advice, including how to deal with your child's school:
http://www.bullying.co.uk or call the helpline for advice: 0808 800 2222
http://www.antibullying.net

National Family Mediation

For separating or divorcing couples. Mediation can help couples make joint decisions about a range of issues.
Website: http://www.nfm.org.uk

Gingerbread

Support and practical help for lone parents and their children via a national network of local self-help groups. Offers advice on child maintenance, employment, education, housing and welfare benefits.
Website: http://www.gingerbread.org.uk
Telephone helpline: 0808 802 0925

Race Equality Foundation

Promotes race equality in social support and public services.
Website: http://www.raceequalityfoundation.org.uk
Telephone support line: 0207 428 1891

Relate

Can put individuals in touch with local Relate centres, which offer counselling to couples experiencing relationship difficulties, including those who are not married.
Website: http://www.relate.org.uk

Samaritans

Telephone helpline and face-to-face service offering emotional support for anyone in a crisis, including those who are feeling suicidal.
Website: http://www.samaritans.org.uk
Telephone helpline: 08457 90 90 90

Women's Aid Federation England

Help for women experiencing physical, emotional or sexual violence in the home.
Website: http://www.womensaid.org.uk
Free 24-hour national domestic violence telephone helpline: 0808 2000 247

Sane

Provides information and support to those suffering mental illness and their families.
Website: http://www.sane.org.uk
Telephone helpline: 0845 767 8000, evenings only.

Carers Line

Advice and information for carers on any issue.
Website: http://www.carersuk.org
Telephone helpline: 0808 808 7777

Winston's Wish

Winston's Wish is a national helpline providing support, information and guidance to all those caring for a child or young person who has been bereaved. The line is open Monday through Friday: 08452 03 04 05.
Website: http://www.winstonswish.org.uk